Being with Rachel

Being with Rachel

A Story of Memory and Survival

Karen Brennan

W. W. Norton & Company

NEW YORK   LONDON

Lines from "On My Third Daughter's First Night Home" by
Jacqueline Osherow, which appears in her collection *With a Moon in Transit*,
copyright © 1996 by Jacqueline Osherow, are used by
permission of Grove/Atlantic, Inc.

The epigraph that appears at Chapter 8 is from *Memory's Ghost* by
Philip J. Hilts. Copyright © 1995 by Philip J. Hilts. Reprinted with
permission of Simon & Schuster.

A portion of this book appeared as an essay in *The Business of Memory*, edited
by Charles Baxter, Graywolf Press, 2000.

For information about permission to reproduce selections from this book,
write to Permissions, W. W. Norton & Company, Inc., 500 Fifth Avenue,
New York, NY 10110

The text and display of this book are composed in Granjon
Composition by Tom Ernst
Manufacturing by Quebecor Fairfield
Book design by Brooke Koven
Production manager: Julia Druskin

Library of Congress Cataloging-in-Publication Data
Brennan, Karen, date.
Being with Rachel : a story of memory and survival / Karen Brennan.
p. cm.
ISBN 0-393-01961-6
1. Brennan, Rachel—Health. 2. Brain damage—Patients—Utah—Biography.
3. Amnesia—Patients—Utah—Biography. I. Title.
RC387.5 .B748 2002
362.1'97481044'092—dc21
[B]   2001051415

W. W. Norton & Company, Inc., 500 Fifth Avenue, New York, N.Y. 10110
www.wwnorton.com

W. W. Norton & Company Ltd., Castle House, 75/76 Wells Street,
London W1T 3QT

1 2 3 4 5 6 7 8 9 0

For Rachel, with All My Love

Great is the power of memory, a fearful thing, O my God, a deep and boundless manifoldness; and this thing is the mind, and this am I myself.

—St. Augustine, *Confessions*

She is our star, what keeps [our family] in this fragile, difficult balance . . .

—Karen Brennan,
"Scenes from the Present," from *Wild Desire*

Being with Rachel

I

I want to begin with a dream I had in the summer of 1995. Because it was a dream with two parts, I entitled it "Dead Girl in Two Parts." What follows is a direct transcription from my journal. *Part 1: a girl in a school uniform falls from a ledge, from between the arches of a wrought-iron railing, to her death. I am sitting on the ledge and my daughter Rachel may have been there as well. The girl falls, I realize, because she is so small and (I think at the time) the wind blows her off. She is simply swept through the railing. When I look down I see her little pile of school clothes—it seems to be all that's left of her. I feel regretful but not horrified.*

In the second part of the dream we—me, Rachel, and the little girl—are at the seashore, sitting on a beach, close to where the waves lap up. Suddenly a large wave washes over the little girl and kills her. Rachel and I look at her face staring up at us from beneath the water. It is a distinctive image, the face of the girl, eyes closed, under the shallow water which moves softly over her. I feel more than regret now; I feel guilt. I feel that one of us (Rachel) should have been more attentive. There is a sense that Rachel had been in charge of this girl. I am therefore a little annoyed with Rachel's irresponsibility, but this isn't a major annoyance. It's more like the resigned feeling I get in real life when someone's done something wrong (as if, for example, Rachel wrecks the car I plan to give her for her birthday) and I realize it's futile to make a big deal over it.

Approximately a month after I wrote this dream in my journal, I received a phone call in my Mexico flat—I had been spending the summer in San Miguel de Allende—informing me that my twenty-four-year-old daughter Rachel had been in a motorcycle accident and that she was presently in a deep coma in Denver General Hospital's intensive care unit. Her friend, the driver, was fine, but Rachel's CAT scan, the informant, a neurosurgeon, told me, was very very ugly.

By eleven that morning I was on a first-class flight from León to Denver, sitting next to a woman who owned a travel agency in Guanajuato. She was pretty, I remember, dark-haired, dressed in cream-colored slacks and a white blouse. She wore a tiny silver watch on her wrist which, because I had lost my own, I had recourse to consult now and again. She was on her way to Denver for a romantic weekend with her husband. We had, what seems to me in retrospect, a pleasant conversation. I told her about Rachel's accident; she consoled me. I did not cry. I spoke reasonably, I thought at the time, having all the while the bizarre sensation that I was speaking someone else's words about someone else's daughter. I suppose I must have been in shock.

I remember that as we conversed my mind raced along another track, somewhat at odds with our conversation. I imagined Rachel, even at that moment, woozily coming to, rubbing her eyes, her sore head. I pictured her fully awake, out of the intensive care unit by the time I arrived, and I planned her homecoming, her few weeks of rest. I even went so far as to imagine my sudden memory of this time—on the first-class flight to Denver, next to the woman in the cream-colored slacks, when I was terrified out of my mind.

My older daughter, Margot, met that Delta flight. My beautiful, usually unflappable daughter looked, I saw immediately, *dismayed*. We fell into each other's arms and, for less than thirty seconds, we wept. I would discover that one could cultivate these fitful griefs, like catnaps—so much more economical than the longer, luxurious spells. Which is to say, right away we knew we would not be able to give ourselves over to the abyss of our worst fears, but had to *pull ourselves together*. I hadn't, until those days, conceived of our family as the pulling-itself-together variety, but here were Margot and I having made a decision to dry our tears and walk briskly to the baggage claim, as she reported the events of the past day as efficiently as a wartime journalist. The coma, persistent, deep, 2 on the Glasgow coma scale; the CAT scan, showing bleeding in the brain itself and widespread injury to the cortex; the prognosis, unknown, gloomy.

"Thank God you're here," she said. "The men are so mopey." The men were my two sons, Chris and Geoff, who had flown in from San Francisco; and two ex-husbands—

Tom, the father of all four of my children, and John, their stepfather. There was Tim, a young man I'd not yet met, the boyfriend, the driver of the motorcycle which crashed for no known reason into a hillside off a long strip of country road in Steamboat Springs, Colorado.

"You should hear them, gloom and doom," Margot said. I could imagine this. The men in our family tended to be fatalists—if only to offset my own, occasionally foolhardy optimism. "They're just waiting for the plug to be pulled." It was a horrible sentence and it shocked me.

In the airplane I'd not allowed myself to think the worst and here it was: We could actually lose Rachel. Margot went on to explain how Chris had been the first contacted by the Denver General staff member. Chris was always changing his residence, and Rachel happened to have his latest phone number in the pocket of her jeans. "Your sister has been in a motorcycle accident and is severely brain injured," the hospital worker had told Chris. "Are you willing to sign a release on her organs?" And Chris had been indignant. "She will need all her organs," he told them. Soon after, he notified Margot in Tucson, then hopped a plane to Denver with Geoff.

But now, overwhelmed by hard evidence—Rachel's failure to respond, the doctors' frank and almost brutal assessments—even the boys, as I still called my grown-up sons, had given up hope. They *were* mopey and particularly hapless as they flipped too quickly through dog-eared copies of *Time* and *Newsweek* in the ICU visitor's lounge. They stood uneasily when I arrived, as if ashamed to tell me what had happened—as if, in their manliness, it had been their duty to prevent it.

We were an oddball clutch of characters. There was ex-husband Tom in his camouflage pants, what was left of his hair pulled into a thin ponytail. For the past five years, Tom had been living in a school bus in the middle of the Sonora desert, somewhere near Sahuarita, Arizona—none of us quite knew where. Now he was manning the pay phone in the visitor lounge. He seemed to have acquainted himself with the array of distraught persons who waited, along with the rest of us, hour after hour, for news of recovery or decline. The pay phone rang constantly and there was Tom, our self-proclaimed receptionist. "Right here," he'd say, and Mrs. Ortiz, whose husband had suffered a stroke, would make her way to the phone, a toddler in her arms. Or Matt, whose brother had been shot in a drive-by. Or Ella, whose son was recuperating from neurosurgery.

Then John, ex-husband number 2 and still dear friend, an attorney, who after the divorce grew his hair down his back and had an ear pierced. Now a silver map of Texas dangled merrily from his ear, in sharp contrast to the worried expression on his face.

Chris and Geoff, tall, handsome, looked like rock stars in their black leather jackets, a few bright chains looped in Chris's belt, San Francisco style. They put their arms around me, and I was grateful for the leather wall of them to put my head against—none of us knew quite what to say. "It's unbelievable," we finally said. "Rachel of all people," we finally said. Because of all of us, Rachel had been the healthiest, the sturdiest, the most intrepid, and, dare I say it? the luckiest. With her sunny disposition, her considerable talent as a competitive distance runner, she was, as a friend of mine once remarked, "biochemically blessed." I thought of this as I tried to muster some faith in her recovery. I reminded myself how

the odds had been stacked against her as a two-month premature cesarean baby who'd needed three exchange transfu-
sions, whose first year in this world was so fraught with peril
that she'd been hospitalized three times—for pneumonia, for
whooping cough, for croup.

Tom's position was that we should face facts. "I've been
through this before," he said, which was true. Our friend
Barbara had lost both of her teenage sons in a single motorcycle accident fifteen years before. She'd had to disconnect their
life supports on the second day, on the advice of her physician,
who pronounced them "brain-dead." During those first
moments in the visitor's lounge, I was haunted by the memory
of Barbara and her decision to let her sons die, the most excruciating decision of her life. Could I let Rachel die? Would I
have the strength and wisdom to know what to do? And that
awful word, "brain-dead," would someone pronounce her so?

I was introduced to Tim, the boyfriend of the moment,
who'd taken Rachel on his motorcycle a short twenty-four
hours ago. A slight young man with a kinky mane of dyed
blond hair, a la the snowboard culture of the day, he shook
my hand frantically and in his eyes I saw real terror. I put my
arms around him, having made up my mind to not muddle
my focus with blame or anger. Then John, looking especially
weary, hugged me. "Let's not give up," I whispered to him,
because I could not imagine our strong, healthy Rachel not
managing to overcome anything.

WHEN I ARRIVED in Denver that first evening, I knew nothing of brain injuries, of axons, of intercranial pressures, of
ventilation or tracheostomies, of motor strips, frontal lobes,

aphasic disorders, or unilateral neglects. I knew nothing of comas. What I knew was what I witnessed in the ICU that night, like a particularly grisly episode from *ER*: bodies being whirled by on stretchers, or corpselike in beds, hooked up to monitors, a nurse with a clipboard positioned at the end of each.

Rachel was one of these bodies. She had a tube running down one nostril (nagogastric) for feeding, another in her mouth (endotracheal) for breathing. A little semicircle of her hair had been shaved above the forehead on the left side, from which protruded a three-inch metal bolt. This was to measure her intercranial pressure. The monitors flashed above her head on a large green screen: heart, respiration, blood oxygen, blood pressure, and intercranial pressure.

Rachel's eyes were closed. She had a small scrape on her cheek. The toes of her right foot were badly burned and grotesquely blistered. Occasionally she moved, but these movements were not reassuring; rather, they were the unnatural movements of one who has severe brain damage, called, in med-speak, *posturing*. At this stage, Rachel's postures were the most severe variety—decerebrate—indicating damage at a deep level of the cortex. They consisted of Rachel flexing her body and limbs rigidly into an extended position, her hands and feet flipped inward in a grotesque way. Every time she postured, her intercranial pressures rose, meaning that the fluid in her brain was increasing to a dangerous level. Eventually, another half-moon of hair would be shaved on the other side of her brow and a drainage tube inserted to draw off the excess fluid and blood.

Margot had prepared me for the shock of seeing Rachel—the tubes, the monitors, the horrible bolt screwed into her cranium, the tubes running into her nose and mouth, taped to her face, almost obliterating it. Sometime after her flight to Italy from Salt Lake City in June, where we'd said good-bye, Rachel had dyed her hair a dark, burnished red. It was a nice color for her, and I found myself absently approving, imagining how well it must show off her bright blue eyes. I gingerly lifted the white hospital sheet and even more gingerly lifted her thin blue gown, and there was her fit runner's body, completely and astoundingly undamaged, not even a bruise.

At around this time, the resident checked in with us. An amiable, soft-faced woman, not much older than Rachel, she took one of Rachel's hands and pressed the tip of her pen into the nail bed of her thumb. Hard. Rachel responded immediately—flexing her arms and legs in a "posture"—though her face (what I could see of it) was impassive, as if the pain had found a pathway around her very being. "Why do you have to do that?" I asked. The resident—I think her name was Maureen—explained that this was one of a number of neurological tests administered to Rachel throughout the day. Her reaction—posturing—she told me, was hopeful. Somewhere, the pain registered. Not brain-dead. Then she pried up each eyelid and shined in a tiny bright light. There, too, a small reaction. I could see for myself the contraction of the pupils, though they were sluggish contractions, said Maureen, not quite normal.

I began to nourish my little seed of hopefulness then, the notion that a few minute signs might add up to a miracle. Moreover, Maureen advised that we try to wake her up. "Talk to her," she said. "Sing, make noise." She told us the story of the comatose Haitian man whose family surrounded his bed in the ICU and chanted and prayed, performing noisy rituals until he opened his eyes. It seemed a bizarre undertaking in a room of critically ill people, each bed separated by a flimsy curtain. But then someone found Rachel's Walkman in its blue fannypack, and I fitted the headphones on her and turned up the volume. Who knows what the music was? Some rap singer she used to work out to, the lyrics faintly obscene. For a few days, she listened to that tape, and, for the record, it did nothing. No more than my endless conversation; Margot quipped that I was tormenting her awake, and we cheered ourselves briefly by envisioning a scene in which she'd come to shouting "MOM, SHUT THE FUCK UP."

But soon enough we knew better.

Hospitals, if they do anything for the families of the brain injured, cannot be accused of not providing them with information. We had more information than we could bear on traumatic brain injury (TBI). Pamphlets which began with diagrams of the brain, arrows pointing to its lumpy hemispheres and, rather simplistic, I would learn, descriptions of their functions; photocopied instructions to the "loved ones" (why did that phrase sound like "the bereaved" to me?)—be patient, expect personality change, memory loss, cognitive deficit ranging from mild to severe; descriptions of rehabilitative procedures, testimonials of recovering head-injured persons; copies of brain injury newsletters from national and state organizations; a chart outlining the stages of coma, called the Glasgow coma scale; another chart referring to stages of recovery, called the Rancho de los Amigos scale. And more—lists of insurance lawyers, nursing homes, home health care organizations, and family support groups, regional as well as national. It was all too much to take in and, frankly, struck me as irrelevant at the time. What impressed us most in those first days was the information that Rachel would not "come to," as they do in the movies. A patient goes into a coma, and when she returns she is changed forever. The wake-up itself had stages that ranged through levels of agitation and confusion. The wake-up would not comfort us; it would upset us.

The attending physician, Dr. Cleary, looked about eighteen: long, ringleted hair, an angelic, slightly bug-eyed face, she could have been a good Mormon wife with her floral dresses and unvarnished nails. I am ashamed to say that she did not especially inspire my confidence and that this, I'm sure, had to do with her age. Nonetheless, she spoke with authority, saying things I wished were not true. She explained, the first time we met, that Rachel had suffered a *diffuse axonal injury* and offered an alarming analogy: "Picture," she said, "the color-coded wires in a phone line. Now picture them sheared off and striving to reconnect. Only in a brain injury the right colors do not necessarily connect up again. Blue may find yellow, red may find green, and some may never reconnect." These colored wires represented the axons that run from the outer layer of the brain to the cortex beneath, linking both layers of the brain and making possible the connection between brain and world, brain and body, brain and self. "We never know what will happen," Dr. Cleary told us. "Except that since her injury was diffuse, her wake-up will be diffuse." It seemed almost too simple to say.

That first night I checked into a room at the Holiday Inn which I shared with Margot, who'd be returning to her children, Nick and Maddy, the next day. I lay in bed, awake most of the night reading the packets of information. It was hard to believe that just the night before I'd been dancing at a Mexican cafe with a boorish real estate man who lectured me on the investment potential of the countryside surrounding San Miguel. At midnight, I'd raced home in a torrential downpour, the large key to the Spanish colonial mansion in which I rented rooms jangling in my pocket. At six A.M. the phone rang; I heard it dimly, as if in a dream, and didn't bother to answer. (The phone was always ringing in my flat, and it was invariably the wrong number.) At eight it rang again and I picked it up. That was the phone call which changed my life, I thought, though Rachel's life had changed hours before, when that motorcycle careened over the hill. I imagined her lying there, "pinned," as someone reported, beneath the bike, unhelmeted, her red Adidas flung fifty feet away, a crescent shape burned into its rubber sole. I tried to imagine her last moments before the accident—had she been laughing or frightened? Did she see what was coming? Did her life flash before her eyes?

LIKE THE BIPOLAR melodrama of a soap opera, those weeks in Denver swung fantastically through crises and denouements, tears and even hilarity. One of the nurses commented to a friend that we were an unusually irreverent family—"it's as if they don't realize the seriousness of what's going on," she worried. "Oh, they realize the seriousness," said the friend, Uma, a doctor herself. "That's just the way the family copes."

Which was true: Our default was the ironic—the grisly fact of the body harvesters across the aisle from Rachel's bed, the pulmonary technician with his choked, breathless voice, the young doctors who soared off on motorcycles with their body-pierced boyfriends—all were occasions of irony and all made us laugh, if somewhat halfheartedly. Otherwise we dealt with each observable second of Rachel's condition, watching the monitors too closely (as one nurse admonished), watching for something to register on her placid, sleeping face.

Strangely, the adrenaline seemed to agree with my body—I was revved up, focused, even calm. And though I was certainly terrified in the depth of my being, on the surface I was in high gear, mobilized and much more efficient than usual. I ran on little sleep, and I finally brought myself to read every word of the information packets, though here my mind went fuzzy; I couldn't take it in, what lay ahead. What I gleaned from all those pages was the following: There were three types of brain injury—mild, moderate, and severe. Rachel's was severe. Yet I persisted in believing that if I did everything right, Rachel would recover. I'd been raised a Catholic, and deeply ingrained in me was the notion that if I only behaved, evil would be averted, good would triumph.

As I write these words, I'm struck by the superman-ish flavor of them, as if some caped individual could come swooping in to restore serenity to our lives. I must have been thinking of the cape of the Virgin of Guadalupe, blue with gold stars, and the Guadalupe herself, renowned for miracles of healing. For the past few years, she'd been a beloved kitsch figure for Rachel and me, Mexico-philes that we were, and we collected her image in figurines and on postcards, refrigerator magnets, and even (for one Mother's Day) a T-shirt.

According to the legend, the Virgin appeared to a young Indian boy, Juan Diego, in 1531. He'd been making his way home in the hills that surround what is now Mexico City, when he was arrested by beautiful music emanating from nowhere and then saw an apparition: Resplendent in her blue-and-gold cape, poised on the crescent of a moon, roses everywhere, the Virgin listened to Juan Diego's request to heal his uncle. She gave him a cloth on which was a likeness of herself so realistic that even an ophthalmologist centuries later believed he was gazing into human eyes. Guadalupe, therefore, is especially linked to the power of her own image; and so suddenly to be surrounded by pictures and reminders and dreams was, in a sense, to be visited by an apparition.

Someone fastened a small Guadalupe holy card to the rails of Rachel's bed, and then my sister in Tucson, out of the blue, began to dream of the Mexican Virgin. It seemed, for a while, that we were deluged by Guadalupes, Guadalupes everywhere in the cards and gifts sent to Rachel and spotted randomly throughout the day: a nurse with a Guadalupe bracelet, a taxi driver with a Guadalupe postcard tucked beneath his visor. Weirdest of all, a prayer to the Virgin of Guadalupe written in Spanish appeared on the windshield of my car where it was parked at the Holiday Inn. And since any sign, from blood pressure to the tiniest tremor around Rachel's closed eyes, *meant* something, I began to pray to Our Lady of Guadalupe. *Let her make it through*, I'd pray. *Just let her wake up. Just let her live. Just let her have her life.*

I WAS READY for a miracle of any sort; I was waiting for one. Whatever skepticism I'd had in my previous life, as an academic, an intellectual, a writer, vanished in the face of my desperation. I was open to anything.

We were visited by chaplains who doused Rachel with

holy water and by new age devotees who gave us totems of
healing to put near her bed—sacred stones, feathers, tarot
cards—and embarrassing rituals to perform over her sleeping body. A Ph.D. nurse from the University of Colorado
instructed me in the art of therapeutic healing, and, with her,
I passed my hands over Rachel's "energy fields," seeking to
perceive the slightest negative vibration. How I would pro-
ceed with this knowledge, I had no idea.

One afternoon, a large man in an electric green suit
arrived in the visitor's lounge. Bidding us rise and join hands
in a circle, this minister from the Church of the Nazarene
began to Praise the Lord in a voice resonant with vibrato. I
raised an eyebrow at John, who was the last person I'd expect
to join in *that* circle. "It can't hurt," he shrugged.

Nothing quite measured up to the Guadalupe for me,
though, and in the months and years that followed Rachel's
injury, it is the Guadalupe that continues to appear to us, in
one way or another, and it is she we credit with our miracles.

In this I was (and am) supported by my mother, an ardent
Catholic, and, more important, one who prays continually.
Retired in Florida, my parents were too old to travel, but I
talked to them daily. My mother was, I knew, praying day
and night for Rachel's recovery. But I longed for my mother's
real presence, for her calmness and faith, for the smell of her
hair and skin. I envisioned her with me, by Rachel's side.
"I've sent my guardian angel to Rachel," she told me, quite
seriously. "I've loaned him to her for a while." And, it's true,
I felt a presence (motherly? saintly?) keeping vigil with me,
now and then, a light-filled spirit hovering over Rachel's bed,
saying *don't give up.*

My father, a retired take-charge business executive, had more practical ideas. At the time, these ideas struck me as impossibly oddball and out of character for my dad, who, for the most part, was skeptical of anything that wavered off the course of middle-class conventions. Chief among these was the suggestion that I contact a doctor who had devised some electrical device which was supposed to jar people out of comas. He had met someone on the golf course who'd known a doctor who'd known someone with a stroke, and so on. But I couldn't bring myself to call this innovative physician with her special machine. Beneath their words of encouragement, my parents' voices on the telephone sounded thin and frightened, the way I must have felt inside.

Meanwhile, Rachel's team of nurses and doctors and medical personnel labored to ensure her survival from one harrowing moment to the next. Rachel's "team," as it was euphemistically called, consisted of her nurses, doctors—neurosurgeons, attending and resident—and a social worker who tirelessly negotiated with insurance companies and that bulwark of terror, the hospital billing office.

The only bright light in those days was the discovery that Rachel *did* have insurance. For the past two years, she'd been living in Colorado, a ski bum, she used to say proudly, who did a variety of menial jobs in exchange for ski passes. Her only real job had come last year, when she was a teaching assistant in a bilingual junior high. She'd quit her job at Basalt Middle School in May, and I was sure her insurance had expired along with it. But, miracle of miracles, the insurance expired on September 1, which meant we had about a week to file for COBRA and all her expenses would be covered.

The caseworker from the insurance company was especially helpful and compassionate and, except for the four-thousand-dollar air-med flight which wiped out my savings, worked hard to get approval for everything Rachel needed.

But the most valuable team members in those days were her regular nurses, those patient, sleep-deprived men and women who sat at the foot of her bed around the clock, monitoring the monitors.

The first days after a brain injury are the most critical—the intercranial pressures can build dangerously and cause even more damage—swelling, bleeding—to the already traumatized brain. Blood pressure can rise, causing a stroke; the heart rate can slow down or speed up, indicating acute distress to the lungs or heart. As it was, Rachel was on a ventilator in those first days—an archaic-looking dun-colored box which, attached to her oxygen, actually forced air into and out of her lungs at a preset rate. It made a sound like a monster in a monster movie, exhaling and inhaling, coming closer and closer. In a week she would "over-breathe" the ventilator, signifying her ability to breathe on her own, and she would be "weaned."

Around the same time, we signed the release for a tracheostomy, and soon her trachea would be punctured through her neck and outfitted for her breathing apparatus, freeing— if only cosmetically—her mouth and nose. It would make her more comfortable, they told us. The surgeon also made an incision on her belly for the feeding catheter, through which flowed the greenish "nutrients" they gave her in those days. Sans tape and the skinny plastic tubes running into her nose and mouth, we could see her face, the quick flitting beneath her eyelids, her lovely, serious mouth. She was who she always was: Rachel. Of this we were sure.

... what eludes poetry:
A long, safe passage through this dense conspiracy
Of unpredictable, marauding danger:
Probably, love's purest form is terror ...
— JACQUELINE OSHEROW,
"On My Third Daughter's First Night"

AFTER FOUR DAYS, Dr. Cleary called a meeting with family members to apprise us of changes in Rachel's condition. We sat in a smallish conference room with high white walls and one window through which a blue patch of sky persisted. I longed for the world of that sky, for the inevitability of each day rising and falling, the gentler drama of the everyday. How could we have landed on this side of things, in an eye blink? It was a marvel to me, an awful marvel, the way a catastrophe could so instantaneously undo our perception of everything.

The family that gathered around Dr. Cleary for that first meeting had expanded beyond the borders of blood and legal ties, former and present. Rachel's immediate family was all there, including Margot, who had returned to Denver with her husband, big blond Steve Kerr, a professional basketball player and Rachel's brother-in-spirit, as well as brother-in-law. Tim's parents, Nora and Ron, had driven out from Kansas to help him through his ordeal, and they sat quietly, nervously, with their son during that first family meeting. In retrospect, I admire their courage.

Bridget, Uma, and Karen Sahn were there, Rachel's good friends, and Karen's mother, Gene Marsh, a Ph.D. nurse at the University of Colorado was there too, as she was throughout our stay in Denver, offering her considerable knowledge and support. John's brother Tom, my former brother-in-law and a nurse at Columbia-Presbyterian, had flown in from New York and was invaluable to all of us with his knowledge of trauma and recommendations for care.

There must have been fourteen of us clustered in that little room, the cheerful sky at an impossible remove behind the one high window, notebooks on our laps, as Dr. Cleary explained the results of Rachel's first MRI. "We have found," she began, "a little blood spot on the brain stem. We don't know what this means, but it's very small, very very small."

It seems to me she repeated this information in a number of ways. "It could have been large, and that would have been a certain disaster. As is, we're not sure what the consequences will be."

Fine, I thought. A blood spot on the brain stem. I could have run around chanting this like a nursery rhyme. *Blood spot on the brain stem.* "Actually," she said, keeping her eyes dulled, noncommittal, "we don't know if Rachel will wake up or not. We may have to make some family decisions."

She was talking about life-support disconnection—I knew it from Barbara and her sons and I wasn't ready to entertain any such notion. I stormed from the room, down the stairs, and out into the smoking area where my cohorts, the usual sorry band of nicotine addicts, were pacing in their hospital gowns, flicking disposable lighters, exhaling almost audibly, as if they could breathe out all the pain and misery that had befallen them.

Denver General Hospital is called, not so jokingly, The Gun & Knife Club. Some of this club's members—gangsters with cryptic faces and oversized jeans—smoked cigarettes nearby. I spotted and fixated on a little crop of dying zinnias. They seemed to be an important, if obvious, metaphor. Some had lost their petals, and their color was scorched to almost neutral in the August heat. They were in concrete beds. A litter of cigarette butts surrounded their stalks. There was no story I could tell myself, no future I could conceive of without horror. At which point a wheezing woman rolling an oxygen tank bummed a smoke from me. She was homeless, she explained, she'd been evicted from her apartment. Now she was almost out of oxygen. I gave her a cigarette and twenty bucks.

I sat in the grass. My thoughts were disorganized, and I needed an idea. I recalled the Buddhist wisdom that impermanence is the true nature of things, and the Hindu adage that everything is *maya*, illusion, that those who are enlightened can pass their hands through the fabric of the world. I thought of Guadalupe and her propensity for miracles. It was then that it occurred to me that Rachel would be okay. I had been looking at the sky, at a particular cloud formation which seemed to be filled with light, and it came to me:

She'll be fine. It will go on and it will change and it will be fine. She will.

I was stubbing out my cigarette as the rest of our group wandered out into the sunshine, looking dazed and shaken. Nora, Tim's mother, made her way to me. "I wish I'd never given birth to him," she whispered. "Oh no, Nora," I said. I was thinking about Rachel, about the last time I saw her, at the Salt Lake City airport as she was about to board her plane for Italy. There she was, sturdy, healthy, excited, her tan leather Ecuadoran backpack slung over her shoulder. I dropped her at the airport's curbside, and this was what I regretted now. That moment at the curb would be the last time I saw that Rachel, the old Rachel—the tough runner, world traveler Rachel with her Ecuadoran backpack, my daughter. Why couldn't I have parked and taken her to the gate? I remember putting my arms around her, saying I loved her, saying good-bye. And that was that. I still have a postcard she sent from Florence, where, she reports, she had a hair-raising ride on the back of an Italian friend's moped.

"It takes more than one to make a reckless decision," I told Nora. Then I told her I knew that Rachel would make it, as if my words could create their meaning in the universe. One thing had become clear to me out there among the smokers: No family decisions would be made yet. In the distance, my sons, Chris and Geoff, shuffled toward us, then John and Tom, the two exes, serious-faced and sad. Then Margot and Steve, who winced in the sunlight, holding hands. This is our life, I thought. This is the novel of our lives. This is our life, flashing before our eyes.

———

THERE WAS A MOMENT, during the first week, that I counted twenty-three people in the visitor's lounge waiting to see Rachel. Or, I should say, *to look at* Rachel, as she lay there in her coma. They sat nervously with cards and relics and books and bouquets of flowers (not allowed); they'd driven in from Aspen and Snow Mass, flown up from Tucson and even out from the East Coast. Some whom I had never met or even heard of wept openly. And two by two they were allowed into the ICU to gaze upon their friend and feel as helpless, I imagine, as any of us felt then.

Rachel had more friends than anyone I knew. I like to tell the story of how, on her first visit to Utah, she ran into not one but two people she knew on the Alta hiking trail. That evening, at Ruth's Diner, she recognized our waitress as her ice cream shop co-worker from high school days in Tucson, and before I knew it she was in the kitchen, whooping it up with the wait staff. Also legendary is that I couldn't walk through the Tucson Mall with her without stopping ten or fifteen times to chat up the passersby. Even in Mexico, the year before, when she had accompanied me, someone called her the new Mayor of San Miguel, as she greeted and hugged her way through the *Jardin*.

Now, in the visitor's lounge, I counted twenty-three people. It was Bridget—"the General," as my nephew calls her—who pointed out to me that we needed some organization and gently suggested that they needn't all see Rachel. As it was, *we'd* had to relinquish our places near Rachel's bedside (the two-at-a-time rule) so the stream of well-wishers could have their chance. Bridget was right, of course; what was the point of any of them hanging over her bed, seeing her in that condition? What could any of them do? And so

we collected the flowers, cards, and gifts and thanked the visitors and resumed our places near Rachel.

By then, I'd begun to perform a few routine nursing
duties myself. Gene instructed me in using the tiny green
peroxide-soaked sponges to swab out Rachel's mouth—
"mouth care," she called it. Ben, the physical therapist,
demonstrated range-of-motion exercises, wherein Rachel's
arms and legs were moved and rotated in order to prevent
contractures, and doing these exercises became a part of our
routine together. An aide taught me to bathe Rachel, using a
pan of warm water and a washcloth. I was grateful that I
could do *something*, that I could help maintain her gums and
limbs, that I could lather and rinse her arms and legs and
belly and the back of her neck.

Margot washed her hair one morning, tilting Rachel's
head back over a bowl and shampooing and rinsing with a
tenderness I didn't think my no-nonsense daughter capable
of. It was during this beauty session that Rachel opened her
eyes and cast them wildly around the room. Her eyes were
off, one looking left and the other right and neither seeming
to register much of anything. The nurse on hand commented,
"inconjunct gaze," a phrase that stuck with me, that even perversely pleased me with its oxymoronic semantics. And the
fact that it *could* be named, this frightening manifestation that
was my daughter opening her eyes for the first time, was reassuring. Because really, with every fiber of my being, I wanted
to tell Rachel, *For God's sake, close your eyes.* Because, really, it
was a terrible sight, our first indication that the wake-up,
indeed, would disturb us. It was so much easier to watch her
sleeping face and believe, having no signs to the contrary, that
her life would continue where it left off.

More alarming times would come when her trachea would collect mucus not cleared from the lungs and she'd be unable to breathe, causing her to gasp and pant and choke. Then the monitors would go off, beeping emergency sounds like a car alarm, indicating she wasn't getting oxygen, and I would fly into a panic unless someone came immediately to suction out the trach. It still gives me chills to remember this procedure: a long suction tube would be inserted into her trachea, now handily exposed at her neck, and she would turn almost blue from the lack of oxygen, thrashing on the bed as her body struggled for breath. To assist the nurses, I often held her down for these procedures, but I had to turn my head and shut my eyes until it was over, until her body calmed and resumed the corpselike sleep of the coma, which paradoxically calmed me too. Once, during a coughing and choking spasm, the monitors ringing like death knells, I screamed for a nurse who screamed back at me: *Don't panic!*

This was the mean nurse, perhaps the only mean nurse in the ICU in Denver. She ministered to Rachel with a brisk, almost brutal efficiency, jamming the suctioning mechanism into her trachea and down into her lungs, pushing her head roughly to one side. She was the only one who complained about us, the "loved ones" who surrounded Rachel day and night. This was the nurse who hissed, within earshot of all of us, "The family keeps watching the monitors." Another nurse, not mean but possibly *tactless,* mused how she wouldn't mind being in a coma and losing all that weight. She was the one who, in trying to explain Rachel's future deficits to us, speculated that Rachel might not, "for example, know the difference between a refrigerator or a car." "Thanks for the insight," I said as dryly as I could, but John said, even more dryly, "Does that mean she'll try to drive the refrigerator?"

After a week or so, the crowd thinned. Margot and the boys went home; John left for Tucson; the friends cleared out, needing to get back to jobs and families. Remaining were Tim and his family, my ex-husband Tom, and Gene, with daughters Stacey and Karen, who lived in Denver. My Holiday Inn room was oddly bereft, though in a way I was thankful for the solitude, and, anyway, before long, my Tucson friend Robin Hiller would brave her fear of flying and join me by Rachel's side. We'd spend all day and much of the evening watching Rachel as she slept and choked and assumed those frightening postures—though the postures had changed from *decerebrate* to *decorticate,* which meant some small progress might be underway in the brain's healing process. In these new postures, the arms and legs would draw rhythmically upward and down instead of extending straight out. If I hadn't known their awful significance, I would have thought these movements almost beautiful, like dance, articulating the body's mysterious, unconscious grace.

I watched the monitors as if watching a spellbinding horror movie. The brain-drain had been removed, and soon the bolt screwed to her cranium registering the ICPs would be removed as well. Intercranial pressures normal, breathing normal, I waited as anxiously for the wake-up as if I were waiting for a child to be born.

When the complications set in, as vigilant and observant as I thought I'd been, I hadn't seen them coming. Overnight, Rachel's fever rose alarmingly and pneumonia set in. "It's never a question of *if,* it's of *when*," the ICU nurses told me.

Everyone in intensive care gets pneumonia. Everyone with a trach gets pneumonia.

By the time Robin left and my friend Toni Nelson arrived to share my Holiday Inn room, Rachel was covered with an ice blanket, which looked like an enormous sheet of blue bubble wrap, through which icy air blew to keep her fever down. Rachel's teeth chattered, even unconscious, her teeth chattered. I longed to hold her and warm her up. At night, Toni and I drank gin, and I thought, This is it, this is my life now. I was trying it out as an idea. Though I really didn't believe it.

EVERYTHING THAT WENT on in those first weeks in Denver seems, from my present vantage, to have taken place not only long ago but in another dimension. I'm amazed that I can recall as much as I do. Though really, how much of any memory is trustworthy? Had there really been decaying zinnias in concrete beds in the Denver General smoking area? And my companion on the flight from León to Denver, had she really worn cream-colored slacks and not, say, a brown twill suit? I can recollect with a Proustian clarity my Holiday Inn room with its green flecked bedspread, the exact position of my giant suitcase in the corner of the room, by the big window, splayed out messily, a summer's worth of clothes and gifts spilling across the carpet: an eerie trace of my life before this one, that life which had become irrelevant, even trivial, by comparison.

There would be an evening when I'd open my journal and discover my transcription of the dead girl dream I wrote a short month ago, which seemed now like a dimly recollected dream from childhood. I was surprised to discover I'd appended a few notes to my account of the dream. I noted that this was an important dream, having been recalled with that special lucidity one attributes to dreams of significance. I'd wondered about the parts of the dream—parts 1 and 2— and wondered why two parts. Were the two parts of my title, for example, a simple reference to the two parts of the dream, or were they, in a Freudian ambiguity, literally two parts of the girl—physical and mental?

Accompanying my dream account and dream notes was a series of sketches. I'd sketched the arches of the railing through which the girl fell to her death, and I'd sketched the girl herself standing under an arch, a stick figure in a skirt. Then I'd sketched the relative positions of Rachel and myself on the ledge, behind the railing, looking down on the little pile of school clothes, which I also sketched. Whereas after my account of part 2 of my dream, I'd made only one sketch, which I labeled "dead girl's face under a wave." The girl's eyes were closed, her hair snaked around her head, the wave replicated in a series of quivering lines, not unlike the surreal bars of some prison. I wrote: *Why a rooftop? Why a ledge? Why two scenes? Why Rachel? Why resigned?* This last seemed to be the most enigmatic; it didn't fit in with my psychological speculations as to the dream's meaning. I had written: *But the dream seems more complex than this.*

Coming upon this account of my dream after Rachel's accident, of course I read it in a new light. Now the dream, absolutely, seemed to be a portent of some kind. Indeed, the sketch of the dead girl's face under the wave struck me as bearing an uncanny resemblance to Rachel's face in her coma. And weren't the lines of water moving across her face, in fact, a brilliant figure for the hazy boundary that separated us at this time, she in her world, we in ours? Such an interpretation defied all that was reasonable and yet was the most "reasonable" of any I could come up with: That is to say, it was able to connect most of the disparate elements into something that cohered. Even the resignation felt so acutely by my dreaming self seemed to name the gray and stubborn feeling welling up in me as each day went by and Rachel failed to wake up.

Moreover, in its grandiose irrationality, the dream-as-portent affirmed a sense I was getting of life's best-kept secret: that like the flimsy curtain surrounding Rachel's ICU cubicle, what separates dream and reality is not so substantial as we might want to believe; that our worst fears hover around us, like ghosts waiting to spring; that the well-wrought narrative of our waking lives might be our civilized attempt to make a civilized dream come true.

But even in the midst of nightmare, the ordinary distracts us, presenting a world where everything is humdrum and unreasonably taken for granted. There was a wonderful dinner at my friend Gene's home—chicken barbeque in her cozy backyard with its well-tended fruit trees and shaggy raspberry patch. At dusk, as two rabbits scampered beneath our feet on the redwood deck, Gene passed around her latest hobby: She was knitting animal fur into little sweaters and scarves. Rabbit, German Shepherd, Siamese, and it struck us as hilarious—I think I laughed until I cried, until I felt my laughter turn to crying, until tears and laughter, whatever they were, seemed to melt into one another, leaving me breathless and a bit baffled.

The same laughter struck one evening when my friend Beth Alvarado (who, like Robin, had flown nervously from Tucson) and I took a cab back to the Holiday Inn and thought we'd be kidnapped by the driver, who'd stopped midway in our trip to allow a young gang member into the car. His head was shaved, he carried, quite visibly, a gun, and when introductions were made, a certain chill entered the interior of the cab. But all I could do was laugh, as if everything in my life had turned into a joke, another turn of the screw, as Henry James had put it, referring to life's unrelenting ironies. Eventually they let us out of the cab—my hysteria may have played some role in our liberation, or maybe it was all the blabbing about my comatose daughter that inspired a sudden sympathy.

Meanwhile, Tim, the boyfriend, curled up on the gray carpeted floor of the visitor's lounge, night after night; he'd borrowed a pillow from the nurses station and an inadequate hospital blanket. In an odd turn, Tim had replaced Rachel or had at least become the part of her we could make better. Tim, whom we could comfort, assuring him of his blamelessness, worrying about his sleeping, his guilt, his psyche. Nora and Ron assured me that Tim had never taken a drink, that he had certainly never smoked pot. But, according to Tom, the police report noted a good quantity of THC in his blood.

However, we weren't prudish about marijuana, and Tim had told us there was a witness to his careful driving; he had her phone number, he said. And she would also testify, he assured us, to the brutal police treatment of him, putting him in restraints and interrogating him mercilessly. Even Maureen, the resident, seemed to join us in the Tim camp.

She told me one day that the accident might have been worse had Rachel been wearing a helmet, that because it was a velocity-to-force-type injury, a helmet's added weight on the head would have increased the force of trauma.

It was ex-husband Tom, with his overtuned antennae, who could not ignore the issue of Tim, the boy who drove the motorcycle over a small embankment when he should have been paying attention. Tom looked on with disgust as we took Tim under our wings. This was the way it'd always been with Tom; we chose up sides. While I sat by Rachel's bed, stroking her hand, her forehead, brushing her hair, praying, talking, singing, Tom was on the phone with the police chief in Steamboat Springs. While I defended Tim, more out of superstition than conviction—I said, "No negativity, not now"—Tom wanted the police to come and take him away. But whatever happened later, I have to admit that the fact of Tim was a comfort to me then. I felt he'd stay with Rachel, which meant he'd be there with us as she recovered from whatever this would be. I felt I owed him the chance to make it up to her.

I felt this with a particular acuity because, years ago, a good friend of our family had been driving a car in which a boy had been killed. The mother of the dead boy had not been forgiving. I vowed I would be. I knew enough about the futility of blame, the way it seemed to shrivel the spirit of everyone it touched. I was looking for an opening, an opportunity for grace. "I've taken so much from you," Tim whispered one day. "Sssh," I said, holding him, "don't say that. She won't be taken."

Meanwhile, week 2½, Rachel cracked her left eye and slid it in my direction. The thumb of her left hand began to caress my hand as I held it. How amazing was her little thumb making that deliberate movement! Her lovely blue eye actually focusing on my face! (Though whether she recognized me I have no idea.) Pneumonia under control, her vital signs normalized, her neurological signs showing "promise," as Dr. Cleary put it, we were now looking for a facility in Salt Lake, something called a "coma stim" unit where she could go until the time was right for an acute rehabilitation program.

And just when everything was on the verge of being settled, Tom began to lobby for Rachel's return to Tucson. Tucson, he insisted, was where her roots were, where her friends lived. True enough, but her friends weren't her mother, argued the doctors and nursing staff. I allowed myself to be furious with his meddling. "You have no rights," I hissed at him after the first "mediation" meeting.

The fact that these mediations had to be arranged between Tom and me is an indication of how ugly our feud had become. Down the hall our daughter lay comatose, while here in a small conference room, flanked by strangers, her parents haggled over her.

And Tom, it turned out, *did* have rights. Though I'd had sole custody of our children, now that Rachel was a legal adult, the next-of-kin shared decision making about her care and treatment. I suppose this was what infuriated me so much. In retrospect, I suspect that our rage was a way of displacing our far greater anger at what had befallen Rachel— what better targets than each other?

Thanks to the intervention of our children, Tom finally signed the consent form to have Rachel air-medded to Salt Lake. He sincerely thought this plan made no sense, and he shook his head sadly as he signed his name. But he'd admitted to the staff that he himself would not be totally available throughout Rachel's long rehabilitation, and I vowed I would be.

These things were decided: Rachel would be flown to Bountiful, Utah, at my expense, to reside in a nursing home until she emerged from her coma, after which she would be admitted to the University of Utah's acute rehabilitation facility. Tim, the boyfriend, would live with me in Salt Lake City. I would *not* ride in the specially outfitted intensive care plane with Rachel and two nurses. Although I was invited on this journey over the snow-capped mountains, I could not bring myself to join my comatose daughter in a tiny plane. The nurses, I explained to someone, would have more on their hands with me than with Rachel. My friend Beth would drive with me from Denver to Salt Lake.

On Day 18, we celebrated Rachel's twenty-fifth birthday in Denver. No cake, just a few silly gifts—a silver ring I slipped on her forefinger, some cards pasted to the bars of her bed, paper flowers from Mexico, a southwestern version of the Virgin of Guadalupe painted on a small, rectangular board from Gene. Tim and I sang softly to her while the sunlight streamed in the windows, a good omen I thought. And I thought too of the car I'd bought for her—a white jeep—which would now go to her brother Geoff. And I thought of the year we'd planned—her studying Spanish literature in the University's master's program and snowboarding on weekends and living with me in my rented house on Third Avenue. And I thought of the last time I saw her and how I never knew it would *be* the last time I saw that pre-accident, intrepid girl with her leather backpack slung over her shoulders, on her way to Italy. And it seemed that her life and mine had shrunk into a kind of funnel shape which lay behind us and that in front of us was something so large and inexplicable that I could not get my mind around it.

Beth and I headed out of Denver and into the mountains on Day 20. Somewhere above the green Rockies—shockingly green in summer, like a dress I once owned—and the fastidious mountain passes, a tiny air-med plane would fly with my daughter hooked up to oxygen and food bags and vital sign monitors. She would arrive the next day, just after us. The big-shouldered, good-natured nurse that tended her had pinned a set of wings to the lapel of her hospital gown. "I've never seen anything like it," he said. "I've never seen a coma patient in REM sleep, but I'm sure she is. I'm sure she's dreaming."

3

For it always happened when I awoke like this, and my mind struggled in an unsuccessful attempt to discover where I was, everything would be moving round me through the darkness: things, places, years.

— MARCEL PROUST, *Remembrance of Things Past*

BORDERED BY THE Wasatch mountains on the east and the silver expanse of the Great Salt Lake on the west, South Davis Community Hospital is nestled in the picturesque valley which is Bountiful (really and truly!), Utah. Consisting of a single redbrick structure with white trim, it looks more like an insurance office building or a Mormon ward than a medical facility. Properly speaking, South Davis is *not* a medical facility; it is, as the words beneath its logo quietly state, a nursing home. There are plots of carefully maintained grayish shrubbery on either side of the wide drive-through, where ambulances pull up leisurely to deposit long-term residents. The few parking places reserved for visitors are nearly always vacant.

Inside, the walls are papered in hues of beige and pale blue and peach. Coordinated wall-to-wall carpeting muffles the sounds of footsteps and incoming gurneys and old wheelchairs with slumped passengers that occasionally creak down the hallways. On the main floor, aside from the therapy rooms, there is a small business office and an even smaller cafeteria, which offers a soup du jour and grilled cheese sandwiches every day of the week, except Sundays.

In spirit and in ambiance, South Davis is the polar opposite of Denver General. Nurses and nurse's aides lounge at their stations, idly penciling in crossword puzzles or chatting on the phone. The more ambulatory patients wander the halls in bathrobes or settle on the blue sofas in one of the recreation rooms (each floor has one) to eat meals or watch TV. There are no sounds of monitors (these are registered as flashing lights in the nurses stations) or ambulance sirens; there is no urgent intercom paging of doctors. Physicians make their appearances once a week.

All in all, I felt there was something chilling about this facility—as if the job of the personnel was to allow each patient to drift peacefully out of this life and into the next. Rachel was given a room on the fourth floor, mostly a pediatric floor with a few coma and Alzheimer's patients tucked into rooms at the far ends of the corridors. As we emerged from the elevator, an undersized child crept toward us in a toddler's walker, her arms and legs deformed and knotted, her face twisted into a grimace, of joy or pain we couldn't tell. Other children rocked on chairs in the rec room, some moaning softly, others staring vacantly at the large-screen TV. An Alzheimer's patient restrained to her wheelchair by a pink canvas strap was trying to break free. When I passed her on my way to Rachel's room, she grabbed my arm. "You were always such a little character," she said.

I am ashamed to say that I was terrified. It was as if the curtain of the world had been ripped open and behind lay this: the unfit, the abandoned, the terminal. That Rachel was among them was unthinkable to me, and I felt my body stiffen as I walked down that fourth-floor hallway for the first time, holding my breath.

Rachel's room was a double, but she was the only one in residence. Compared to the makeshift quality of the ICU cubicles in Denver, it was impeccably clean, almost as if unoccupied for several years, and, of course, quiet. A large double window overlooking another brick edifice and some far-off trees in the Wasatch foothills offered a pleasant enough view, and the pink-and-blue wallpaper edged with a pale scalloped border was soothing, almost too soothing. I found myself wondering how they planned to stimulate Rachel out of her coma.

Rachel was already situated in the bed by the window, hooked up to trach apparatus, humidified oxygen, and her g-tube (food) catheter for her bags of nutrients, which had changed from green to brown. Her equipment gurgled and hissed around her, as if she were at the center of an elaborate but absurd machine. She was diapered. I'd been thrilled to know that here she'd be allowed to wear her own clothes—I suppose I thought shedding the hospital gown signified a step toward homecoming—and I'd spent a little time that morning shopping for new nightgowns and sweats and T-shirts. We even had slippers—Chris had sent them: green, fleece-lined, like elves' shoes. And Nikes and socks, which I'd found among her Italy clothes.

She was wearing the Denver ICU gown, which I removed, maneuvering a new pair of pajamas, gray with pink checks, around the tangle of catheters and monitor wires. I took charge. It was as though that war zone in Denver had certified me to take charge. I brushed her hair, her teeth, and ran a washcloth over her face. I even changed her diaper. Later that day, I helped the aide bathe her in an actual tub, easing her underwater and steadying her shoulders as she floated unevenly, betraying, I supposed, her body's utter helplessness. The aide sprayed her with warm water and washed her with a sudsy cloth, and it seemed to me that it must feel heavenly to be in that tub after three weeks of gowns and beds and traumas. Indeed, midway through the bath, Rachel's left eye cracked open and slid toward where I was kneeling beside her. Was she looking at me? I had no idea.

THESE DAYS, STORIES of comas are in the air (or do I have my ears cocked for them?). Not only the stifling South Davis air, but the real air of the media and TV news. A man who's been in a coma for nine months suddenly wakes up, walks across his hospital room, and peers out the window. A six-teen-year-old emerges from her coma after a year and is now attending her high school classes. She's doing very well in math. These stories fuel my hope at the same time that they fill me with foreboding. Nine months? A year?

Rachel *seems* to hear me. But I have no idea if she knows me. She squeezes my hand, twice for yes, or is it twice for no? I am uncertain if she's being deliberate or if I'm making things up. Plus, *I* can't seem to keep our codes straight.

Nevertheless, she opens her fingers very slowly and squeezes and then repeats the motion. Therefore (I convince myself) she is saying she hears, she understands, she knows. But her eyes—her eye—show no recognition, and her face is as blank as a wall. *Coma coma coma.*

The Glasgow coma scale is an assessment tool used to measure the severity of comas. The scale measures responsiveness along three variables: eye opening, verbal response, and motor response. According to the experts, the Glasgow scale has "a high degree of interobserver reliability," which means that most observers of a coma patient assessing these variables agree with each other. The scale also is reputed to "correlate well with outcome following severe brain injury" and therefore is considered to be a predictive tool—the worse the score, the longer the bad score, the worse the outcome. According to the Glasgow scale, Rachel was a 2 upon admittance to the intensive care unit in Denver and now, in Utah, she was barely above a 2, and only in two variables: her motor responses were slightly more advanced, and she seemed (though who knew?) to open her eye in response to pain and/or discomfort. Her verbal score was 1, nonresponsive, completely and utterly. There was no doubt now that her brain injury was severe, that it would have severe consequences for Rachel for the rest of her life.

An alternative assessment is the Rancho de Los Amigos scale, an eight-point measurement of response, from a comatose "no response" to an almost fully recovered "purposeful-appropriate." On this scale, Rachel was solidly between a 1 and a 2, between what they call "generalized response" and "localized response"; that is, she reacted inconsistently but occasionally (or so it seemed to me) specifically.

Now, my life is ruled by these measurements, by reading and re-reading the very specific and, at the same time, maddeningly vague descriptions of levels of consciousness. For "generalized response," for example, "a patient reacts inconsistently and nonpurposefully"; and for "localized response," "patient responses are specific but inconsistent"; and for level 4, "confused-agitated," which is what we aspire to these days, "patient is in a heightened state of activity and severely confused, disoriented, and unaware of present events."

I watch my daughter for hours each day, taking note of the smallest flicker of her thumb or mouth or eyelid, taking the most minuscule of signs as a portent of hope. Like a scientist bent over a microscopic specimen, I feel that my vigilance is crucial, that without it she might slip away into some uncharted and doomed territory. It's like those times when the airline pilot announces that, on account of air traffic, he will assume a holding pattern above some city, and it feels like a terrible eternity before the plane is able to land safely. Or those last weeks of pregnancy, the maddening wait, the anticipation, and the terror. There is a measure of excitement in our vigil. In retrospect, I understand this excitement to be a product of our refusal to believe that the worst will happen. We cherish the expectation that we will eventually land safely, greatly relieved and in a celebratory mood.

Days into the South Davis ordeal, a parade of solemn visitors begins. First Chris, my oldest son, flies in from San Francisco a few days after Rachel is admitted to South Davis. A few years ago, Chris had been the victim of a brutal gang beating in front of a convenience store in Tucson. The long scar along his jaw, which had been broken in four places, recalls that interminable night in the emergency room,

Chris's beautiful, angular face so swollen he was unrecognizable. He and Rachel share similar coloring, blue eyes, dark hair, as well as a kind of ferocity of spirit. At the moment, Chris's jaw is set and hard as he watches his comatose sister. I briefly entertain the notion that, by sheer force of will, Chris, the most intense of my children, will be able to call her back from coma land. He glowers at the nurses, but with his sister he is tender, tears filling his eyes. Outside the building, I give myself over to my own tears, sobbing as I hold onto the dull brick of the building. Chris grabs my shoulders from behind. "Let's go, Mom," he says, turning me toward the car.

When Chris leaves after a few days, I am bereft. But soon my sister Mary Pat will arrive from Tucson. Mary Pat spends days in South Davis, wandering hospital corridors by my side, sitting by Rachel's bed. We try to laugh at the ambiance. Mary Pat, a decorator with great wit, is especially disdainful of the scalloped-edged wallpaper that trims the hallways—and we both decide we love the meals in the cafeteria, the Campbell's tomato soup, the veggie platters copiously laden with marshmallows, the lard-iced chocolate cake. The woman with Alzheimer's has been parked in the hall outside Rachel's room: "D-E-F," she shouts to any who pass her, "A-B-C." The Alphabet Woman, we call her, not without sympathy. "If that ever happens to me, will you promise to tweeze my chin hairs?" asks Mary Pat. Later, wistfully, watching Rachel's freckled face with its sheen of sweat, she confesses, "I never knew why you called her Rachel. She's much more like a Molly." We both look on in a companionable silence, as my indeed Irish-looking daughter flutters her eyelids.

Tim moves in with me in the middle of September. He'd been back to Steamboat to pack his belongings into his black

SUV, and he'd sold the motorcycle, thank God, for two hundred dollars. Actually, there is much less wrong with the motorcycle than there is with Rachel, I am chagrined to know, only a few dings and alignment problems, like a sprained ankle. He pulls up to the curb in front of my house on a Friday, and by Saturday, we've transformed my basement room into a cosy, if windowless, retreat for Tim.

There he installs his plaid Lazy Boy and his home-made bong collection. I have to laugh. His parents went to great lengths to assure me not only that Tim had never smoked pot but also that he'd never had a beer. Nora and Ron certainly never had a beer. There was a night in Denver when they'd insisted on taking Beth and me to dinner at a famous franchise Mexican restaurant. It was one of those convivial, annoying places where all the waitpeople dressed up as giant animals. Before the meal, Ron had us join hands and pray. After the prayer, I put in my order for a Corona.

But here is Tim with his bongs and his Lazy Boy, inordinately proud of each, knowing me rightly as a nonjudgmental ex-hippie who'd probably seen her share of bongs. As it happens, the bongs are an annoyance. But sort of as I would a mosquito buzzing intermittently overhead, I don't give them my full attention. And frankly, I need Tim's support. I swat away the fact of the bongs and my growing misgivings. Whenever I feel my anger aiming in Tim's direction, I remind myself of my vow to be forgiving and compassionate—as if such reluctant generosity would score me points with fate.

I should mention that I have a driving phobia and that the drive to Bountiful is virtually impossible for me. In his memoir, *Experience*, Martin Amis observes that most poets don't drive and those that do shouldn't. Because I'm at least half a poet, Amis's pronouncement grants me a kind of reprieve. For years, my driving phobia—unclear even to me, characterized by unbidden panic attacks and unpredictable driving-range demarcations—has made me ashamed. Now the phobic demon in me has decided I cannot manage the drive to Bountiful, even, and perhaps especially, under the present circumstances. And so I am dependent on Tim's driving expertise. You puzzle out that irony; I am too desperate to give it a thought.

He is desperate, too. The Steamboat Springs police set a court date for him—the charges are reckless driving and driving under the influence—and he counts on me to write a letter in his favor. There is still that witness, he assures me, who would testify that he'd been driving safely, that the police had brutalized him at the scene of the accident, that there'd been some kind of telephone company equipment in the road. But when I ask about the witness now, he gives me a vague answer. Couldn't really find her. Lost the phone number. But told a friend of someone who knew a friend of hers that—et cetera. He is sure she'll call soon.

Every day for weeks, Tim and I drive to Bountiful along route 89, past the rigs of Commonwealth oil, the smoke-stacks which spew eerie orange and blue flames against the mountains at twilight, reminding me of that surrealist '80s film *Brazil*. Tim thinks so too, and I have to admit it is nice to have him there, in these early days, someone to chat with, to commiserate with, someone as invested and responsible as I am—or so I believe at the time.

Tim becomes an expert at the technology that surrounds Rachel. He is able to hook and unhook her oxygen, adjust her trach paraphernalia as professionally as a nurse, and even change her bags of nutrients. At around this time, she begins to sweat profusely, mainly on her face and brow. I use a stack of white washcloths to sop the sweat up, and no sooner is one saturated, than big fat globules bead up again and turn to rivers streaming down her forehead, cheeks, and chin. I am told that in brain injury the temperature mechanism in the brain often becomes impaired and that patients may feel intensely hot or cold. I am told that this was a phase of comas, on the way to a wake-up. I am told that the condition is temporary, perhaps due to the infusion of humid oxygen into her trachea. In other words, no one quite knows why Rachel sweats.

The nurses, or more often the nurse's aides, wander in every few hours to check her temperature, her diaper, her bandaged foot. It's a far cry from the care she received at Denver, and, so far as I can tell, there is no coma stimulation.

Unless you count the therapies, which begin almost immediately. Rachel is lifted to a type of wheelchair, a leather recliner with wheels—with her at a measly 110 pounds, this is no great feat for anyone—and transported to the physical therapy room on the first floor. There Patricia, the head physical therapist, and her assistants go through the range-of-motion exercises with Rachel and even try (unsuccessfully) to get her to sit on the edge of the vinyl therapy bench, propped up by two therapists and me. More like a giant rag doll than a twenty-five-year-old former athlete, she is unable to hold up her head; it hangs down over her chest while long strings of drool slide from her open mouth and onto her sweats. But her left eye is wide open during these sessions and seems, as time goes on, to contain a small seed of fury in its depths.

One afternoon, Rachel defecates in the middle of a therapy session. Shit oozes out of the sides of her diaper, runs down her leg, and puddles up on the vinyl therapy floor. I am humiliated for her, almost apologetic, despite the therapist's no-nonsense competence with a new diaper and a handful of paper towels. For a moment, I glimpse something larger than both of us, Rachel and I, larger than our own tragedy: for this is what it means to be human, to be animal, to be sick. At the root of all of us is this indignity—and the real healers among us are not distracted by it.

After a few weeks, a Poe-like device of torture called a "tilt table" becomes part of her routine. The tilt table is a long board with a narrow platform at one end and a hand-operated crank along one side. Rachel is strapped onto the table; then the table is cranked until she is standing on the platform below. The purpose of this procedure is to stretch her heel cords, which have become shortened during her long sojourn in bed. Heel cords that are not routinely stretched in coma patients require surgery down the line, when, presumably, the patient becomes ambulatory. The table is cranked to 45 degrees, then 90 degrees, and Rachel is standing almost upright for several minutes until the heart monitor registers her discomfort by a flurry of tachycardias (fast heartbeats).

For all of these activities, I am her entourage. The rest of the time, I lie beside her in bed, holding her, talking to her, saying whatever comes to mind. Singing *Wake up little Rachel, wake up* and other inventions too embarrassing to mention. I recite her life story to give her some context for herself, but she seems confused by all of us. (Though how would we know? Even confusion, presumably, is decipherable, and Rachel is not decipherable at all; she just lies there.)

I tell her the story of her life *as if* she can hear me, *as if* she needs to know. What I don't remember, I invent. I feel it's more important to deliver a coherent narrative than to be faithful to a disjunctive truth. If I were lying there in some kind of netherworld, I'd want a story that made sense, whose points A and B and C were nicely connected. Above us the steady *beep beep beep* of the monitors and the hiss and gurgle of the breathing apparatus and alongside of me this sleeping girl, so beautiful in sleep that I can read anything onto the *tabula rasa* of her face.

MARGOT AND STEVE fly in from Tucson with Nick and Maddy right before the start of the NBA season. They rent a car and come straight to South Davis. I am so relieved to see them I almost burst into tears. Margot is as shocked as I had been at the chilly ambiance, the kids in walkers and wheelchairs, the absence of parents, the terminal feeling of the place. I can see it in her face, though she doesn't say anything. I remember being a young mother and dreading stories of kids who were abused or injured—as if paying attention to such accounts would give them more credibility in the world.

Steve is no stranger to tragedy. His father, Malcolm Kerr, former president of American University in Beirut, was assassinated in 1984, and Steve, then a University of Arizona sophomore, was not permitted entry to Lebanon to attend the funeral. Steve is a rangy, freckled-faced guy with a modest Huck Finn–type demeanor—in a later season, Bulls' fans would dub him "Opie." If I had to order a son-in-law from heaven, it would be Steve. He's funny, smart, a terrific father and husband, as well as sensitive and perceptive.

It was only three months ago that we had a conversation about Rachel on the way to a Tucson restaurant. "You know," Steve had said, out of the blue, "Rachel is the nicest person. She's such a good person." In fact, Rachel and Steve share not only athleticism but a similar spirit—that good-person-hood which Margot used to complain makes everyone else look like a schmuck by comparison.

Steve is grieving like the rest of us. He stands by Rachel's bed holding ten-month-old Maddy in his arms, his face a little paler than usual, stricken. Nick, at three, is busy in the rec room watching sports on TV, already a master of the remote control. Rachel had been a devoted, though somewhat intrepid, auntie. I recall too vividly the time she took him on her ten-speed when he was still in diapers, sans helmet, some kind of big white hat flopping around his amazed-looking baby face. Now he toddles in every once in a while, jumps on Rachel's bed and shouts in her ear: "WAKE UP RACHE! COME ON AND JUST WAKE UP, WILL YA?" Then, having received no satisfaction, he toddles out again.

It isn't long before Steve's presence causes a stir in the hospital corridors. He is besieged with requests for autographs, autographed balls, Bulls' caps, and so on. Always good-natured and generous, Steve spends hours entertaining questions in the rec room and then in the quarters of two quadriplegic teenaged boys. He even gives away a few tickets to the Bulls-Jazz game scheduled for November.

Margot and I stand by Rachel's bed, still monitoring what monitors are left. I can tell it's beginning to be too much for

Margot. She is unusually silent. Finally, she murmurs, "She looks so beautiful." Then: "Hey Rache, you're thinner than all of us." But her voice lacks the spunk of her words. We rub some facial goo on Rachel's cheeks and rub it off again. Rachel's left eye slits open, then closes.

Margot has spent the past few weeks scouring the Internet for information about brain injury. It was Margot who found me the brain injury list-serve, who downloaded and coordinated files of material on coma and medications and rehab facilities. Of all my children, Margot is the most gracefully competent. Picture her under the bathroom sink with a wrench and a flashlight while, in the next room, a group of sports fans are glued to the TV. Now picture her emerging from bathroom grit unscathed, movie-star perfect, the way you'd imagine Michele Pfeiffer would look under similar circumstances; and the drain is flushed. That's Margot.

Since Rachel's accident, we've spoken every day, often more than once. Now her lovely blond hair falls across one eye as she leans over her sister. She sighs deeply. With her marriage to NBA Steve, Margot's world has become invulnerable, like a fairy tale. Here is the part where it all turns sour. Her sister and best friend is lying in a coma. And there's nothing any of us can do except wait. Eventually, she leaves the room to check on the kids.

When Geoff arrives at the beginning of October, Rachel is doing a lot better. She keeps her left eye open almost all the time (except when she's sleeping—coma patients actually sleep, have sleeping and waking cycles). She made advances this week—I was going to say *big* advances, but to anyone who isn't watching the minutiae of her progress, they will seem small. She's moving her right side at last—even, a little, the fingers of her right hand (and I've been worried about that hand). She touches things—my face with incredible gentleness, feeling each of my features with the fingers of her left hand, and last night she reached for a bottle of lotion I was holding, took it from me, rotated it, and seemed to examine it with her one eye.

Moreover, her face has much more expression, though the expression is wrenching, desperate. She actually smiles a lopsided smile at Geoff as he bends over to bestow a brotherly kiss on her brow.

At twenty-seven, Geoff is the closest in age to Rachel, and, perhaps for this reason, they've always been great pals. When he was a cherubic three-year-old with a mass of white-blond curls—as opposed to a tall, handsome guy with a receding hairline—Geoff used to ask in his surprisingly deep voice if he could watch the baby Rachel for me. And that's the way it's always been—he keeps an eye on her. When she moved briefly to San Francisco after college graduation, she lived with Geoff in his Scott Street flat.

Geoff is a bass player. He actually makes a good living as a musician, and he is frequently overbooked. It's hard for him to get away and so I'm especially grateful for his presence now. If you believe the stuff they say about birth order, it is Geoff, the third, who holds the spot of the caretaker. He is everyone's favorite sibling. He hates confrontations, loves nothing better than to cheer us all up with a good joke. Now he's trying with Rache. "Hey Stinky," he says to her, "remember when I used to give you free shots on your head? You want a few now?" Rachel—is she actually looking him?—seems to smile again.

That night, we eat dinner at the Oasis in Salt Lake City. For some reason, there's a big table of us—Geoff and his girl-

friend at the time, Michelle, as well as some of my pals from
the English Department—Srinivas, Ranjii, and Tom. My
friends have been trying to get me to go out more, but I can't
bear to socialize. When the hospital and school days are over,
I want nothing more than to lie in my gloomy bedroom and
stare at the ceiling and drift off. Company at this time seems
almost like a sacrilege—something like, "How can I go out
when my daughter is lying in a coma?"

But tonight, here I am, in honor of Geoff's visit. My
friends look happy: beautiful Ranjii in her silks; Srinivas, like
an Indian prince slumming in his leather jacket; friendly-
faced Tom, his hair pulled back in a ponytail; then Michelle,
a doll-like Vietnamese woman with a great laugh; and my
own Geoff, drinking Amstels, abstracted.

There's a guitarist, a woman with a pure Mary Chapin
Carpenter kind of voice, and I listen to her dreamily, while
around me folks chat and laugh. Then she plays that old
Paul McCartney song "I Will," and I feel the grief building
up in waves, so much so that I beat a retreat to the empty
patio and give myself over to an explosion of choked, rasping
sorrow. Geoff follows, pulls me to him, rubs my back as I
weep and weep. "It's the song I sing to her each day," I
explain between wet gulps, and then I sing a little of it in a
shaky voice. Geoff is Geoff, my steady comfort. Finally, as
quickly as it came on, my grief tunnels out of me, as if I'd
been visited by a flu. When we return to the table, Geoff
actually has me laughing over something.

A COMA IS a "liminal" state. *Liminal*, a word resurrected by
contemporary anthropology, refers to borders and thresh-

olds—that territory *in between* other, more definite territories. A coma, therefore, is somewhere between waking and sleeping, between sleeping and death, who knows where? *Where?* is precisely the impossible question to ask in regard to comas—*where* is the coma, and, more crucially, *where* is the person who inhabits the coma? (Or is it the coma that inhabits the person?)

The first six pages of Proust's *Remembrance of Things Past* describe this kind of uncertain space, where the borders of consciousness are blurred by sleep and dream: The young Marcel "struggles" to awake, and in those moments, "things, places, years" move around him, indistinguishable, unorganized, in the darkness. Proust even speculates that it is only the rigor of our belief that makes the objects of the world fixed and immobile in waking life, as if waking life is a dream created by our immobile concepts of it.

Perhaps, then, Rachel inhabits another reality, I muse, as I lie beside her. Maybe even a *realer* reality, more true because unlimited by our representations of it. In such a liminal state of being, isn't anything possible? For days and days that stretched to weeks, I watched her comatose body and occasionally convinced myself that her soul was wandering someplace else. To bolster my magical thinking, a friend telephoned from Mexico to say he'd seen her in a dream, flying in the skies above San Miguel de Allende and she told him she was fine and she would reenter her body soon. Do I believe this? Do I disbelieve? What I know is that we'd all been transported somewhere *else*—somewhere of which the coma was only a symptom—and in this new place, the presumptions of the old life had come apart.

As a fiction writer, I believe in the power of the stories we tell ourselves. The way each of us chooses to look at the world becomes the world we look at. When you think of it, this is what constitutes belief, even theologies. But what story could I tell myself now?

One night I rented a video from our local new age bookstore, *The Golden Braid*. The video featured Ram Dass and Stephen Levine, both gurus of the new age, holding a seminar for AIDS patients and their caregivers. It would be, I knew, a good antidote to the grim brain injury books and articles I'd been surrounding myself with. New age thinkers can be quite creative in dreaming up ways to sustain our confidence in the world; in the best of this thinking, that which is not dependent on corny oversimplifications, we are offered what in the '70s we called a "paradigm shift," a new way of looking at a (sometimes hopeless) situation.

This video—whose name I've forgotten—offered me comfort that early October night in 1995. Go-with-the-flow Ram Dass was telling a story about caring for his stepmother, who was dying of cancer. To paraphrase loosely, he said that to pacify her with falsehoods about her death would have been dishonest; and to encourage her to hold onto her life would have been unrealistic and controlling. What he could do, and what he advised the seminar participants to do, was simply to *be* with the other person, wherever she was in the process of her illness.

As I recall this advice, from a perspective of five years post–brain injury, it still resonates with canny wisdom. At the time, it struck me as a worthy goal. If I could only situate myself by Rachel's side, *be there*, as those "things, places, ideas" whirled around her in the darkness, then I would be doing all I could. At the very least, Ram Dass's advice gave me a way of believing there was *something* I could do, something that rendered me not totally helpless, but open to destiny, whatever it was. I would, I vowed then, *be* with Rachel, wherever she was and as long as it took. Thus, *Being with Rachel* has become both my mantra and my title, a way of being in my life.

4

At six weeks post-accident, Rachel is more solidly in phase 4, confused and agitated. She's moving constantly when awake. As a kind of greeting, she raises her left leg and plops it on the shoulder of whoever happens to be around. And she plays catch with the stuffed bunny John gave her. She catches it with her left hand and gives it a halfhearted shove toward the thrower. Now she holds onto her trach tube—the hose of humidified air attached to the trach—and occasionally tries to yank it from her neck. Also her g-tube. Worrisome. I had to authorize a restraint on her left wrist (a little cuff that we tie to the side of the bed, which now has pads so she won't hurt herself thrashing around). It killed me to do this, to restrain her in any way. My own body feels agitated, restrained. And I feel that her sadness is my sadness. Sometimes I don't know which one of us is which.

The coma is a state of being that blurs the boundaries between sleeping and waking and dying. Indeed I felt myself falling into the liminal, so to speak, confusing the borderland between Rachel and me. I remember studying Freud's pre-Oedipal phase in grad school, the developmental stage when the infant feels her body to be part of the mother and even vice versa. I can still remember nursing my babies and feeling there was no clear boundary between us. Everything about this phase of motherhood reinforces that feeling: the letting down of milk, the baby's mouth on the mother's nipple, the rocking chair prop that simulates the amniotic sea in the womb. And now, here I was again with that same light-headedness, the sensation that my body's boundaries were dissolving. Rachel had become my baby again.

Twenty-five years ago, two and a half months premature, she was only three pounds and covered with blond fur—it looked more like fur than human hair to me, as if I'd given birth to a kitten. Her head was the size of an orange; her white eyelashes flickered to reveal a tiny, intermittent glimpse of eyes the color of water. Her fingers grasped mine through the holes in the incubator. She had a tube running from her arm to somewhere. In those days, I was afraid to look.

And now, in her room at South Davis, my limbs would become oddly heavy, my movements lethargic, my thoughts dreamy and unspecific, as if I were floating somewhere above my own life. I'd stare for hours at the shadows of the mini-blinds on the wall or at a peaked corner of her white hospital blanket. I began, quite unconsciously, to assume Rachel's postures, only in reverse, as in a mirror image—my left hand stiff and curled by my side, my right thumb moving over hers in a reciprocal gesture.

Moreover, as I recounted her life to her, my endless, repetitive narrative, parts of my life mingled weirdly with hers, just as the outside world seemed to take on the sensual attributes of this inside, hospital one. I spent, on the average, eight hours by—or more usually, in—her bed, and so I suppose it was reasonable that during my infrequent ventures to that other world, espresso machines would sound like the suctioning apparatus for her trach, and someone's beeper would send a rush of alarm through me.

Rachel, it's me, Mom, Karen Brennan (I add ridiculously). *You are Rachel Elizabeth Brennan, and you were born on September 5, 1970. You are the youngest of four children. You are now twenty-five years old. Margot is thirty, Chris is twenty-eight, Geoff is twenty-seven. Margot is married to Steve Kerr, who is a point guard for the Bulls. This year, for the first time, he'll be playing with Michael Jordan! Margot and Steve have two children, Nick and Maddy—sometimes Nick calls you Chake and me Mok. Chris and Geoff live in San Francisco and are both musicians. I teach creative writing and English at the University of Utah. You are twenty-five and are about to enter a master's program in Spanish at the University of Utah. You were planning to live with me. I am not married to your father, Tom, or your stepfather, John, anymore.* (Should I elaborate these painful and complicated stories? Better not.) *You were in a motorcycle accident with Tim. Tim is okay. You have a traumatic brain injury and now you're in a coma. You are a great runner. You speak Spanish. You graduated from the University of Arizona.*

For many years we lived in Tucson. You just moved from Colorado. You spent this past summer in Florence, Italy. Whereas I spent the summer in San Miguel de Allende. (At this point, I imagine her mind hazing over in a confusion of geography, if indeed she is attending at all to this muddle of factoids.) *We love you.* Blah blah blah. *Wake up please.* Blah.

When I look back on this time, it seems extraordinary to me that I believed so absolutely in Rachel's recovery. Certainly, no signs pointed in that direction. True, she was emerging from her coma; true, she had been an athlete, strong, fit, nondrinker, nonsmoker, a college grad, a "success"—in med-speak, she had a great "pre-morbid profile"; true, she had family support. But what really did we have here? A partially opened left eye that only seemed to focus here or there; a few gestures that may or may not have been voluntary. Under oath, I would have had to admit that I wasn't sure of anything.

I came to call those who didn't share my optimism—who felt it their duty to inform me that the prognosis was grim and that I should face facts—the False Hope Cops. The False Hope Cops were everywhere. They eyed me sadly and shook their heads. They looked away when I bragged about Rachel's progress—the bunny game, the left leg greeting. They were the realists. A social worker, whom I came to call the Queen of the False Hope Cops, summed it up best when she said, "Be prepared for the worst; then when something good happens you'll be surprised and pleased." But that's not how I want to live my life, I explained to her. I was an enigma to the False Hope Cops.

Meanwhile, the world was going on, as it does, heedless of our individual troubles. I used to look at people walking along the street or eating in restaurants or passing by in their cars, and I would wonder if any of them had troubles of their own. I doubted it; everyone looked too carefree. But every once in a while, I'd spot someone with a look of secret sorrow, a look I recognized. In the hospital everyone had that look—the patients and the visitors, that is. Sometimes it seemed the nurses had become inured to our hardships; they were breezy or brusque or faintly distracted, bored. Even when they were openly sympathetic, their sympathy had a terrible edge to it, since it was really pity they felt. In retrospect, I understand their skepticism about brain injury recovery, but at the time it struck me as the worst kind of bad faith.

During this time, I attended a brain injury conference in Park City, Utah. I'd heard about it from some of the nurses, who were offered credit and a day off for attending. I sat with them for lunch, and after the keynote speech, which was delivered by a brain injury survivor, we were joined by a young brain-injured woman and her caregiver. She was about sixteen. She walked with a bad limp and her right hand was clawed with spasticity. She spoke haltingly, slurring her words, but she was clearly intelligent and eager to be listened to. She spoke of her plans for courses at the community college, how she was interested in psychology, and she told us about her injury, which had happened when she was an infant. I told her—and meant it—that if Rachel recovered as well as she did, I'd be very happy. Out of the corner of my eye, I caught the nurses looking at me with that pity which passed for sympathy. What did it mean? That they thought Rachel would never be this functional? That they thought this level of functioning was a pathetic aspiration?

At length, I asked the girl to give me some advice. "As one who's been through this whole thing, what advice would you give to the mother of a brain-injured daughter?" She shook her head, then said with some force: "Just don't hit her; hit a pillow instead." I glanced at her caregiver, who was staring into her ice water, noncommittal. Hit her? I thought, amazed. And though I would never hit anyone, it was my first inkling that tough times were ahead.

AT THE END of September, my classes resumed at the University of Utah. My colleagues and friends, back from their summer vacations, sprang into action on my behalf. I'd been at the university for only two years, but it felt as though I were surrounded by family. It was not unusual to come upon Meg or Ranjii or Srinivas or Tom or Kathryn or Jackie sitting by Rachel's side in the hospital, talking to her the way they'd seen me do, holding her hand. I used to call them all Rachel's Team, which would have pleased Rachel, my jock girl. If there were occasional False Hope Cops, there were many more of Rachel's Team to keep us going, to keep *me* going. If at times I felt lost in an ocean of bewilderment, there were those good currents—my friends—who never stopped bolstering me with their generous gifts of love and time. At the end of the day, we'd compare notes: Rachel smiled at Ranjii, she squeezed Tom's hand in a particularly insistent way, Kathryn accompanied her to the therapy session I couldn't attend. Rah rah rah!!

As director of the creative writing program, I was teaching only one class, an upper-division fiction writing class. Twice a week, when my class met, I would give them an update on Rachel. I'd tell them about the lotion bottle or about her new way of greeting people by plopping her leg on their shoulders or about how she smiled—a flash in the darkness, like an infant's rare smile. It was the first and only time in almost twenty years of teaching that I had a Margot, Chris, Geoff, and Rachel in one class—the names of all my children. I took it as a good omen.

Write a story about the hardest thing that ever happened to you; or write from the point of view of someone you hate; or write a story based on a dream; or write about the event that changed your life. . . . This last exercise was a new one for me. I never believed much in event. Event meant plot, and plot, I always thought, was the basest form of narrative. But here I was encouraging event, even plot—and I found myself analyzing my former resistance. I suppose, until now, I hadn't thought it possible that events could change a person: Change came from within, was a product of character and inspiration, a gradual shift in perception, like the slow action of tectonic plates, created by a person's hard look at the world. Now I knew differently.

It turned out to be one of the best classes I ever taught. Why was that? Was it because I was obviously vulnerable and students, like anyone, are good people? Even as the heating vents clanged in the old building and someone banged on pipes in the next room, we all had the feeling that something extraordinary was going on in our room. Whatever it was is hard to define. No doubt, it was my time-out from suffering and uncertainty and frustration, that room full of eager, gifted students: a kind of untouchable place. For a few hours each week, I could forget my real life and abandon myself to another wonderful one—one which, oddly, resembled nothing so much as my "boring" past.

As a creative writing director, however, I was less effective—administrative work is not my forte, and it was simply too much to attend to. To my colleagues' and grad students' credit, they were immensely patient with my shortcomings as an administrator: I would forget appointments, foul up the dates for readings, lose phone numbers. My office became littered with mountains of handouts, books, departmental meeting agendas, RPT guidelines, faculty senate ballots, calendars, invitations, visiting writer profiles, plus their books and bios—stuff that would make my head spin when I rifled through it. One afternoon, I put my head on my desk and wept. It was all too much and I had no idea what to do about it.

To make matters worse, our visiting writers series was beginning, and, as creative writing director, I was responsible for hospitality. Our first writer, a journalist of national repute, arrived hours late on a flight from New York. Tim had driven me to the airport and waited those long hours until the plane landed. I spent the time wandering into the glass-walled smoking section, amid a torrent of eye-tearing nicotine, and wandering out again to check on the status of the flight with a crisply dressed airline clerk.

Finally, the journalist, a person I did not know personally, emerged through the arrival gate cranky and exhausted. I spotted what must be him—brief-cased, bespectacled, unmistakably aggravated—and for the time it took to deliver him to his hotel, he ranted about the inconvenience he had suffered at the hands of the airline. "My daughter's in a coma," I told him, inelegantly interrupting his flow of complaints. "I myself have been waiting for hours at the airport." I felt extremely aggrieved, as if no one else was entitled to suffering but me. As it turns out, the journalist was unfazed and tried to persuade me to join him in the hotel jacuzzi. "You've got to be kidding," I said, as I practically flung his duffel bag at the doorway of his room.

The next night, at the reception held at my house (was I crazy?), the journalist lounged on my bed surrounded by attractive female grad students. This man, I should add, was an insensitive exception to our visitors that year.

Still, the coma and my obsession with it were wearing me out. Both seemed interminable, as if we—Rachel and I—were caught in some suffocating enclosure (a moth trapped between screen and window might be a good analogy), where we could only bat our wings in futility. Sameness. Drone. Imprisonment.

At Margot's prompting, I logged on to the brain injury list-serve and began a communication with a woman who called herself "Sal." Sal also had a daughter who'd been in a coma, but now she was home, watching comedies, laughing with her mother. She walked with a walker, but she'd lost all her friends. She had terrible problems with dizziness and balance. Her speech was slurred. Sal was generous with her time and information, but it was the coma I was interested in, not the aftermath (a worry I'd gratefully tackle if the time came). Also, I found I was not a great Internet correspondent: too self-conscious and, frankly, too busy.

A group of us women, all friends, gathered one night at Rachel's bedside to perform our own version of coma stim. Kathryn played the guitar and sang a song she had composed; Jackie chanted something soulful in Hebrew; Shelley burned some herbs reputed to be stimulants—sage and nutmeg; Meg brought feathers. I did my therapeutic healing thing, learned from the nurse in Denver. Rachel was very still throughout our ceremony, as if she had composed herself for the occasion. There was a feeling of immense goodwill in the room. And though it may have been silly—who knows if these things are silly or not?—and even irreverent, considering my comatose daughter, I felt that our combined love and good wishes were shooting healing vibes to Rachel. But while Shelley was burning a clump of sage and wafting the fumes beneath Rachel's nose, the nurse arrived, visibly upset. Who could blame her? We were lighting fires in a *hospital*. But the fire turned out not to be the problem; the staff actually wondered if we were smoking pot. "Oh," she said when Shelley explained the stimulant properties of the sage. "Oh, excuse me," and she left the room.

There was a general feeling in South Davis that Rachel's family and friends were giving her extraordinary support. I was told over and over how beneficial it was to the patients to have family surrounding them, how it actually improved the prognosis, how Rachel was so lucky to have me by her side.

While I'm sure that was true, it occurred to me that the understaffed nurses were enormously relieved when a parent was able to take over their duties, which is what it amounted to: By this time, I bathed Rachel, changed her diaper, and monitored her monitors, and Tim, as I said, was an expert with all the apparatus, including the changing of the food bag. We couldn't manage the trach suctioning, which continued to frighten me so much I always had to look away as the nurses plunged the suctioning tube into Rachel's trachea; nor could we take care of her burned foot, which, to the nurses' credit, they attended to religiously, that is to say every few days, with quite spectacular results—no loss of toes (only toenails) and minimal scarring.

Outside our room, the life of the hospital moved on at a snail's pace. Patients without visitors were lined up in the hallways, presumably so they could keep each other company. They sat strapped into their wheelchairs, their heads lolling to one side, in various states of consciousness. At the end of our corridor, a young man sat facing the window. Like the other patients, like Rachel, his clothes were new looking, *inhabited* instead of worn: a black T-shirt, black sweatpants with a white stripe, sparkling Adidas shoes, baseball cap. His outfit was a clue to the person he had been—a high school kid, probably, athletic, popular. He was big, broad-shouldered, and dark-haired and must have been handsome. Now his face was distorted with spasticity; both hands were clawed and strapped to splints to contain the spasms. Like the others, he drooled, and when he spoke, if you could call it speaking, incoherent grunts emanated from his chest bypassing the action of his tongue, which was, no doubt, paralyzed. On weekends, he was visited by his grandmother, an elderly Hispanic woman who sat with him by the window, her hand over his knotted, clawlike one. I remember thinking that he was, at least, conscious and that gave him an edge over Rachel. This was the first of many appalling comparisons I would make as time went on.

Billy, across the hall, seemed far better off than Rachel. A big guy, twenty-seven, drug overdose, he was found in a motel room after eighteen hours of injecting something like rat poison, which he thought was heroin. One afternoon, he asked me to help him outside and to smoke a cigarette with him. In his room, I tried to get him out of bed. First, I strapped on his sandals, velcroing them over his white socks. Then I pulled the wheelchair to the side of his bed. "I can lift my own weight now," he told me proudly. But when I tried to move him, he wouldn't budge. He groaned with the effort, as did I. (This, I would learn later, is classic lack of insight, common in brain injuries.)

Finally, I rustled up a few male aides to shift his 213-pound weight and push him to the balcony, where we smoked. I lit a Marlboro and put it in his mouth, and he held it in his teeth as he chatted away. He told me he would propose to his girlfriend when he began to walk again. His arms were badly injured from lying on the motel floor for so long: Part of his right arm had been surgically removed, leaving an enormous hole about a foot long and several inches deep on the inside of that arm.

Suddenly he began to shiver and asked me to get his green jacket. Foolishly, I left the cigarette in his mouth and rushed to his room; when I returned, the cigarette had fallen on his T-shirt and was burning a rather large hole. Billy seemed not to mind a whit, testimony, I supposed, to his affable lack of awareness. But I wondered anxiously if this was a prognosis for my caregiving talents? I envisioned headlines: *Distracted Mother of Brain-Injured Daughter Burns Up Stroke Victim; Says She "Just Spaced Out for a Minute."*

Billy, however, would make a good recovery. Within months he'd be home, walking and with-it. Jared would not be so lucky. Jared, at six, weighed twenty-five pounds. He had been found as an infant, abandoned in a park. Shaken baby syndrome. He would never leave the nursing home. He sat in his wheelchair with his impossibly thin arms in splints and gazed at the ceiling with his cloudy, smushed eyes. When he heard a noise, he rotated his head and smiled a kind of smile: He opened his mouth very wide and made a tiny roaring sound in the back of his throat. His teeth were yellow nubs. Behind the roar, occasionally, there was a child's voice crying out. When I could, I crouched beside him and rubbed his arms and his face. Once in a while, I'd take him into Rachel's room because he was so often alone. I would hold one of his hands and one of Rachel's and pray to Guadalupe to relieve each of them of their sufferings.

One Saturday morning, I arrived later than usual to find Rachel among the lineup in the hallway, legs and arms bound to splints, looking, on the whole, anguished and uncomfortable. Since the only pleasure she seemed to get was her left-side exercises, I was enraged that she had been tied up in this way. I practically assaulted the poor aide in charge, berating her for strapping Rachel down. Why? I kept asking. The poor woman, who barely spoke English, shrugged her shoulders. Clearly, it was a matter of convenience and of habit. All the patients were parked in the corridors, strapped down; this way the small staff of nurses and aides could keep an eye on them. And I suppose it was a measure of my own denial that my protest was so vehement: Surely Rachel was not like these others, most of whom were living what was left of their lives here in South Davis. Surely Rachel would recover.

ONE EVENING I assisted the young male aide who'd come to get Rachel ready for bed. I'd been about to leave, but something about this guy gave me pause. Rachel lay on her sheet, naked, so vulnerable in her coma, so thin. In a period of six weeks, she'd lost her sturdy athlete's body: I could count her ribs. It was clear, nonetheless, that she was a beautiful, young woman, with breasts and pubic hair. The aide, I sensed, was leering at her. I felt a chill go up my arm.

"Will you be taking care of her tonight?" I asked.

"Don't worry, ma'am," he said, "I'll take *good* care of your little girl." Unbelievably, he snickered.

I marched straight to the nurses station. "Who is that guy?" I demanded to know.

Mindy, the nurse in charge, shrugged. "He's new."

"Do me a favor, Mindy, don't let him near Rachel."

"He *is* kind of creepy," she acknowledged.

"Just don't let him near Rachel, okay, Mindy?"

Later that night, I telephoned. On the phone, Mindy confided that he was actually doing his community service.

"What's that supposed to mean? He's some kind of criminal?"

"I'm not sure what he *did*," she said defensively. But she assured me she'd assigned someone else to Rachel. Still, there was a long night ahead, and who knew what could happen in that understaffed hospital? *I should have stayed, I should have stayed, I should have stayed.*

There is danger everywhere—that's what this kind of life-changing event impresses upon us. Is it my own hysteria, my own hyperawareness of danger, that allows this young man—in my mind I call him The Predator—to haunt me throughout Rachel's recovery? Months, even years, later, I will wonder if he harmed her in any way, if her recovery has been impaired by some violation of her body. I will never know whether anything happened or didn't happen that night—or even if I've remembered The Predator correctly or invented him as a convenient object of hate, a place where I can fix all the horror of this nightmare. I should have stayed. Instead, I curled up in my big bed and read more about the atrocities of brain injury.

I'd taken out about thirty books from the medical library at the University of Utah, and what I read would alternately depress or elate me. *Age, pre-injury personality, and family support are the biggest factors in brain injury recovery.* Elation! *One-parent families don't do well with brain-injured family members.* Depression. *Psychological problems tend to beset those who have a tendency toward same.* Elation! *The longer the coma, the worse the prognosis.* Depression.

I studied diagrams of the brain; I learned that the right and left hemispheres are not nearly so distinct as everyone thinks; that research on brain injury was always uncovering new ideas about how the brain is actually organized. There was even an article in a popular magazine which claimed that PET scans revealed that men's and women's brains operate differently—female brains being more "holistic" than the more focused male brain, where functions are keyed to discrete areas and where the hemispheres, indeed, are more precisely divided.

More usefully, I learned that brain injury rarely leaves its victims with physical disability, but that personality change frequently occurs; that violent outbursts of anger are commonplace in brain injury; that everyone with a brain injury has cognitive and behavioral deficits of some sort. The Denver nurse who'd told us Rachel might not know a car from a refrigerator was referring to something the books call "feature identification." A woman goes to a grocery store, in one anecdote, and can't seem to assemble the features of the different foods she wants to purchase. I pictured this woman standing dumbfounded in the produce aisle. Would this be Rachel?

I stacked the books in tall towers on the floor alongside my bed. As I read them, or more accurately, read *in* them, I'd put them on the bed next to me, until after a while I'd doze off surrounded by big, hard medical texts, pages marked with old envelopes or rubber bands or paper clips, whatever was handy. "Unilateral neglect" refers to a person's completely ignoring one side of the body, treating it as though it doesn't exist. "Aphasia" describes a failure of language—either expressive or receptive language—and many brain-injured patients frequently have trouble with both forms of language. Somewhere in the course of all this reading, I realized that brain injury deficits were as varied as DNA, that there was no way to predict Rachel's particular outcome, and so my reading, in a sense, was a bit futile at this stage. Still, I plowed on.

Now, for the first time, I read stories of memory deficits—the short-term memory is the last type of memory to recover in brain injury (and so the recovering brain injury patient is not unlike an Alzheimer's patient for a while), but it usually *does* recover. A few exceptions include the man who would chat amiably with his caregivers, even play chess and golf, and not remember any of what he'd done at day's end. These stories about memory held a horrible fascination for me. I remember thinking, "But Rachel could never have *that* deficit." Memory deficit of this severe variety is usually associated with alcoholism or botched surgeries, said the books. So I ruled out severe memory deficit, gratefully and, as it would turn out, rashly.

AT TIMES, THE VIEW of the Great Salt Lake seemed a great tease to all of us at South Davis, the short- and the long-term residents. Just a view in the distance, beautiful and unattainable as the poignant tattoo of *freedom* I spotted on a young patient's arm. For me, there had always been about the place the feeling of a prison—the spirit of a prison—a place where people were condemned and from which it was almost impossible to escape.

As Rachel's "scores" improved, I took to visiting the University of Utah's acute rehab facility. Despite an air of murky dilapidation—old rooms bathed in yellow fluorescence—there was a bustling energy about the place that encouraged me. I was given a tour of the industrious therapy rooms, the rec room with its recovering patients, biding their time with games of Scrabble and checkers. Families were around too, laughing, sharing meals, shouting encouragement during physical therapy sessions. Eventually, I was introduced to the head of rehab, an silver-haired physician with a warm smile. After listening sympathetically to my incredibly overdetailed report, he informed me that Rachel was not yet ready for the University hospital's program. Despite her roving right eye, her agitation and movement, her eloquent left hand, she was technically a 3 rather than a 4. And, really, a 5 is what was required for acute rehab. She had to be able to tolerate and benefit from at least three hours of therapy a day. At this point, she could tolerate about ten minutes before her heart would begin to race and her blood pressure rise dangerously.

Patricia, our wonderful physical therapist, and her young, warm-hearted assistant worked diligently with Rachel. Her assistant, Gail, called Rachel "Girlfriend" and since then that is Rachel's name for everyone post-TBI. I occasionally wonder if she picked it up when she was comatose in South Davis, going through her range-of-motion exercises. Coma patients hear things, I read. They know more than we think.

Her speech therapist was gloomy in his prognosis for Rachel. He tried, unsuccessfully, to wean her from the trach, by replacing the air hose with a red button that was meant to flap open with her exhalations. But Rachel simply couldn't breathe on her own yet. Likewise, the occupational therapist would visit her bedside on occasion and, after working a bit with her arms, would shrug and leave the room. Once I told him that she really could do more if he gave her the chance.

Patricia prescribed Inderol for Rachel, a drug that would help with the spasticity in her arms and legs. But the Inderol made her drowsy—it seemed, to my untutored mind, to plunge her deeper into a coma and, for that reason, I was against it. The doctor, a young resident who was not a brain injury specialist, saw Rachel for about five minutes a week during which time he looked her over briefly. He didn't touch her, simply looked at her with a slightly worried expression and then turned to the therapists for their reports.

Not surprisingly, the doctor took Patricia's advice and kept up the Inderol. And all the hopeful signs—the hand squeezing, the bunny game, the good focus of the left eye—

stopped. Rachel probably went from a 3 to a 2 again. But at least her limbs were less spastic. From Patricia's perspective, this was a good thing. She was working to get Rachel on her feet, and she actually succeeded in maneuvering her into a weight-bearing position. "If we can get 'em to stand, we can get 'em to walk," Patricia told me.

But I couldn't help feeling that the therapists were ignoring the forest for the trees. What was the point of standing up if you were still unconscious? Finally, I buttonholed the doctor during one of his weekly visits:

"I thought the point was that we're trying to get Rachel to wake up," I said. In response, I got that same worried expression, which might have been his version of bewilderment.

"She's really out of it," I said.

"She's in a coma," the doctor said finally, and without a trace of irony.

Yes, but. I made of myself a general pain in the ass, until finally they lowered her dosage and she began to show signs of life again.

Meanwhile, I kept up my mission at the University hospital. I felt it imperative that she get out of South Davis. We needed to escape—that was how I looked at it. I pleaded and begged. I even donned a black suit and business pumps, in the hopes that my respectable appearance would give me more authority. The doctor in charge finally consented to send a team to evaluate her for rehab. "It must have been quite an outfit," quipped Margot, long distance.

———

Rachel raised her leg and put it around my neck and caressed my cheek with her toes. She smiled when I sang "Moon River" to her. Probably in derision.

Rache kissed my hand and I cried.

Rache stood up with help!

Rache pulled her trach mister hose off its socket and was spraying her face with it when I went in today. Over the weekend, she found her g-tube and chewed on it.

She is finally, finally at level 4 plus—confused, agitated—and is constantly moving. She pulled me down to her chest today and stroked my hair, tucking it behind my ears in a very reasonable way.

When word came that the evaluators had okayed Rachel for acute rehab at the University of Utah hospital, I went out and bought myself a new, outrageously expensive, hat. It was green felt with a grosgrain band, and I went to a dollar photo-booth and had my picture taken wearing it in four different ways. That afternoon, I allowed Rachel to chew on its brim. She was chewing on everything in those coma-emerging days, so why not my celebration hat?

"We're going to a new hospital," I told her. And I told her she'd get better and then she'd come home and then I'd take care of her. I told her we'd go to Mexico and rent a big house and go snorkeling and drink Margaritas and buy clothes from the J. Crew catalogue. I told her she'd indeed attend the graduate program at the University of Utah and teach Spanish 101 to undergraduates and that she'd learn to snowboard. I told her that all of us would be together for Thanksgiving and that we'd have so much to be thankful for. I told her it was confusing now, but soon everything that was spinning around her in the darkness would begin to make sense again. I told her she'd wake up and the world would be as she had left it. I told her all my dreams.

5

"Hope" is the thing with feathers—
That perches in the soul—
And sings the tune without the words—
And never stops—at all—
　　　　—EMILY DICKINSON

I AM STILL visited by this day: We are driving from Bountiful to Salt Lake in the Red Cross ambulance, Rachel strapped onto a narrow stretcher, hooked up to life supports, and me at her side, belted into the yellow plastic pull-down seat. Through the square, blurred window at the rear of the ambulance, a gray day fades quickly into the distance: The trees are mostly leafless and the murky, no-color sky appears to be farther away than usual. Even the cars and buildings we leave in our wake seem curiously dim, as if part of another, disappearing life. Through the ambulance window, the familiar drive has taken on the quality of a home movie—already the subject of nostalgia and past, definitely past tense.

In the midst of this late October gray day, the ambulance siren is on full blast. I put myself somewhere else, outside looking in at us, we who so disturb the landscape, we in medical crisis on our way to the hospital, sealed off from the humdrum world. Would anyone ever guess that herein lies a brain-injured twenty-five-year-old, emerging from a two-month coma?

Rachel is struggling. Both of her eyes are wide open in obvious terror. Her legs have been strapped down along with her torso, but she's able to move her left arm, which she does, grabbing fiercely at her trach tube. I reach over and hold her hand, which spares the trach tube but does not erase the frightened look in her eyes. The ambulance bumps and lurches, swings violently left and right. When it finally screeches to a halt, Rachel is drenched with sweat. But at least we're here, at a real hospital.

Now she's being schlepped from stretcher to stretcher, now she's being whisked to her third-floor semi-private room and unceremoniously tumbled into a bed in the far corner. At no time do her eyes close; at no time do they lose their look of panic. In her bed, she thrashes wildly. "Is she always this agitated?" asks the nurse on duty. "Definitely not," I say. When I look at my hands, they're trembling.

The room has three other inhabitants, all spinal injuries. In retrospect, it seems as if they all had their TVs on. One is knitting as she watches *Oprah*. Another is entertaining a group of family members. The third is talking loudly and enthusiastically on the telephone. Rachel continues to thrash. Her heart rate and blood pressure are elevated, and her trach needs suctioning; she's coughing and choking as she whips her head from side to side.

At this inopportune moment, an old friend of Rachel's makes an entrance. Fred is a tall, earnest young man who happens to be passing through on his way to Moab. "This is not a great time," I say as gently as possible. But the old friend will not be deterred. He bends over Rachel and talks to her in a loud voice. "IT'S ME, FRED," he says. Rachel thrashes.

The resident, Dr. Peterson, arrives almost immediately. Sweet-faced Dr. Peterson will turn out to be a great support to us during our time at the University hospital. Even now, he examines Rachel with tenderness and compassion. But he directs his inquiry to Fred. "Is she at all responsive?"

Amazingly, Fred attempts to provide the doctor with an answer. "Actually, I think she knows me—"

"Excuse me," I interrupt, "I am the mother." Dr. Peterson looks surprised.

I explain that she will squeeze hands, twice for yes, once for no. But when he asks her a few questions, it's clear she is too overwhelmed to respond. Her eyes are practically rolling back in her head, and I fear she might have a seizure, one of the few brain injury effects she's been able to avoid.

"She can't stay in this room. It's too much for her," I say. Dr. Peterson says he'll see what he can do. Fred leaves after a prolonged one-sided conversation during which Rachel thrashes.

As the day wears on, I'm able to persuade the nurses that she needs a quieter setting; mercifully, they free up a private room for the next day. In the meantime, we're stuck here. I pull the green curtain around her bed and pray for morning.

When it is quite late, a young aide arrives with a portable toilet. Rachel is diapered, but the aide informs me that they—whoever "they" are—want Rachel to try to pee in the toilet. Fine. Rachel has calmed down and I guess we're game. The aide boosts the floppy and, at this point, dead-asleep Rachel onto the pot, which is attached to a plastic frame and is, thank goodness, level with the bed. She asks me to hold Rachel while she pees, and then she leaves the room. Keep in mind that Rachel is hooked up to humidified oxygen and a g-tube. There seems to be an impossible tangle of wires and tubes, and I'm having trouble steadying her. She flops, she slips partway off. It is dark-ish and I can't see very well. I am trying to boost her back on the pot and somehow she is caught—therefore we are caught—in this precarious position. It is too much for me and tears sting the corners of my eyes. I can't do this. I can't put my daughter who weighs only 110 pounds back onto the goddamn toilet. I can't even reach the bell to call for help without dropping Rachel. After what seems like hours, but is probably only five minutes, the aide reappears, apologetic. Of course Rachel doesn't pee. She doesn't even wake up.

NOT ONLY HAD Rachel been given a private room, but a nurse had been assigned to her around the clock. The nurse settled herself into a chair at the foot of the bed with her knitting needles, from which something long and red dangled. (It's funny the details that bubble up from the vat of long-term memory; I remember noting this enigmatic handiwork, vaguely curious, but not curious enough to ask, apparently.) Rachel's charts were arranged on the tray table—blue and green file folders, a medication chart.

The nurse, a middle-aged Middle Eastern woman with a roll of black curls grazing the top of her starched collar, had drawn the blinds and turned off all but one small light. She sat with Rachel in the semi-darkness, knitting needles clicking ominously, as if keeping vigil by a corpse. To her dismay, I opened the blinds, turned on a light. "Hi Rache!" I said. "Ssssh," whispered the nurse, "she's in a coma." "Yes," I whispered back, "but the goal here is to wake her up!"

The room was tiny and seemed to be a perfect square. The smallish window gave out on a view of the brick wall of another building, but there was an angular patch of bright sky visible just beyond the edges, symbolizing, I believed, our own small ray of hope in the distance. (I had reached the stage where everything had become a metaphor and I was undaunted by clichés.) It was very peaceful in the new room; the private nurse had nothing to do but attend to Rachel's every need. And knit.

Bliss, I thought. Without Tim, who had gone to Steamboat Springs for the week, or other family members around, I'd felt the full weight of responsibility lately, and a kind of loneliness had lodged inside of me, coupled with misgiving—could I do this? Could I be Rachel's mother *and* her advocate *and* her daily caregiver *and* teach my classes *and* direct the program *and* clean the house? I crawled into Rachel's bed, where, worn out by the commotion of the day before, she lay still for a change, perhaps sleeping. Even so, she found my hand and squeezed it. I whispered in her ear. "You're okay now, darling, everything will be okay."

Eventually it became clear that as long as a mother was going to spend her day at her daughter's side, there was no need for the private nurse to actually *sit* there. Truthfully, I cherished my time with Rachel, and having another person in the room made me self-conscious. But it was a tremendous comfort to know that someone was looking after Rachel when I wasn't around.

That first day in the private room, the fact of the nurse allowed me to attend an educational group for family members of brain-injured patients. When I walked into the small meeting room, a few minutes late, the ubiquitous model of the brain was being displayed for the five or six people who were sitting around the conference table. A social worker was identifying the hemispheres and lobes to the group, who looked on intently. An irate father, wearing a jacket and tie, accompanied by his wife and daughter, was especially worked up. He interrogated the social worker about his son's headaches, fatigue, and mild forgetfulness post-injury. He was told that these were the usual effects of brain injury and would, in his son's case, probably clear up soon. I couldn't help being jealous. The father, on the other hand, was furious with the world; his wife and daughter cowered next to him. A small woman with gold-rimmed glasses took a few notes on a yellow legal pad. When she asked a question about her husband's seizures, she was rudely interrupted by the irate father.

Finally, I described Rachel's coma-emerging agitation and asked if anyone had any wisdom to share with me. "How long has she been in a coma?" asked the social worker. "About two months," I said. This information was met with a stunned silence. Even the irate father cocked his head incredulously before he started in again. No one answered my question.

Soon I would discover that most of the brain injured in acute rehab had comas of much shorter duration and so had milder deficits to deal with. Rachel, with one exception, was the most severely brain damaged in acute rehab. The exception was a woman who'd been in rehab for over a year. This was a pretty redhead who was strapped into a custom-made wheelchair, whose hands and legs were splinted, severely spastic, and who was unable to communicate or move at all. She had been in a car accident and had lost two of her children and her husband. I remember wondering what she had to live for. She was visited regularly by an aunt who, in hopes of stimulating her niece's will to recover, pushed her throughout the long corridors and grounds of the hospital for hours at a time.

After the meeting, I bundle Rachel up in a jacket and her furry leopard hat, buckle her into a reclining wheelchair, and take her for a walk.

There's a story behind the hat. We were in Neiman Marcus (aka Needless Mark-up) in Chicago, visiting Margot and Steve last Christmas, when Rachel fell in love with an absurd-looking and costly fake fur hat with a leopard print. "I really, really want this," she told me. "You can't be serious," I said. It was very large, for one thing. It kind of jutted up from Rachel's head, making her look a little like a Dickens orphan.

"I'm totally serious," she said, her blue eyes flashing beneath the furry brim. "It's the only thing I want for Christmas." So I bought it for her.

Now, I'm glad I did. Something about it is so silly, so *Rachel*—also, it's warm. It's a nippy fall day, but glorious—the leaves are gold and red on the maples, and the spectacular mountains, which we view from the hospital grounds, are actually snow-capped.

I push her along a little path bordered with marigolds. On a whim, I pick one and present it to Rachel. She holds it in her left hand, twirling it, smiling faintly, then, before I can stop her, happily stuffs it into her mouth and begins to chew. I have quite a time dislodging it from her mouth, but, like the hat, I can't help but admire the spirit of the thing.

That afternoon, Rachel met her doctor and therapists. Her attending physician, Dr. Frank, is a physiatrist, a rehabilitation physician whose patients typically include not only the brain injured but stroke and spinal injury victims. A stern-faced woman wearing no-nonsense khakis under her doctor's whites, she barely glanced at me. She was making her rounds with Dr. Peterson that afternoon; when she got to Rachel's room, she riffled through some manila folders and read the chart somberly. Rachel was still in the wheelchair, parked by her window with its view of brick wall and sliver of sky.

"Does she try to talk? Mouth any words, anything?" Dr. Frank didn't look at me when she asked this question; in fact, at first I couldn't be sure she was addressing me. It was Dr. Peterson who glanced my way inquiringly.

"No," I admitted. "But this is because we've told her not to try to talk. I think she understands us," I added hopefully.

"If she doesn't talk, she doesn't understand you, Mrs. Brennan," she said, and she left the room with Dr. Peterson following. At the door, she murmured to him in what was almost a stage whisper: *Aphasic.*

She is not aphasic, I said to myself. And we had told her not to try to talk in South Davis. We'd said: "Don't try to talk with a trach, you could hurt your throat," which is what we'd been told.

This was my introduction to the roller-coaster ride of acute rehab: the depression and elation cycle—or, more accurately, incredible, mind-numbing despair alternating, occasionally, with a sliver of hope. Dr. Frank was probably the Empress of the False Hope Cops.

Next we met the therapists assigned to Rachel, who, I am thankful to say, were a warm and highly competent group of women. There was Molly, our vivacious physical therapist, the best of all the PTs, according to one doctor I knew, who told me, "If my daughter was in Rachel's shoes, I'd want her to have Molly."

Molly worked tirelessly with Rachel throughout her four-month stay. "Hey Rache!" she'd say each morning, greeting her like an old buddy. Of all her therapists, Molly reminded me most of pre-injury Rachel: thin, athletic, and full of cheerleader energy. I found myself fantasizing that they'd be real friends in the future. Even that first day, Molly prodded and pushed, getting Rachel up on her feet, boosting her over the medicine ball, coaching her through a few sets of exhausting leg lifts. You could tell they were exhausting by Rachel's stamina, which was fading fast—and this after only fifteen minutes of PT.

Back in the private room, as we waited for Sandra, the speech therapist, I held up a choice of my home-made "mood cards." In South Davis, I'd made a series of index cards with the most primitive of stick figures. The figures had big round faces with my version of basic expressions, which I labeled accordingly: ANGER, BOREDOM (which was hard to convey), SAD, HAPPY, TIRED, FUNNY, and then YES and NO and MAYBE. In South Davis, this "game" had been pretty much of a bust, but now it seemed that Rachel might be ready to work with the cards. Sandra thought it was a good idea, too. And Rachel did point to the "mood" cards, but whether or not she pointed purposefully at that stage, I still don't know. Certainly, I took her responses seriously—all that day, she pointed to SAD, for example.

Speech therapy covers a broad spectrum: breathing (and so things connected to the tracheostomy) and swallowing, as well as all aspects of physical speech rehabilitation (pronunciation, articulation) and cognitive rehabilitation (itself a category which encompasses many subcategories, from object identification to abstract thinking and remembering).

Sandra, a diminutive, hiply dressed Japanese American with incredible patience, was a master of all of these. It was she who set our primary goal—the removal of the trach—who, in the coming months, would work long hours performing miracles. For the first time since Rachel's injury, I felt that we had a professional team on our side.

Her occupational therapist was Wendy, wonderful Wendy, who would eventually reinstate Rachel's table manners and habits of hygiene, and for now worked on her upper body, mainly her arms and hands. It was becoming increasingly clear that Rachel's right arm and hand were severely incapacitated, despite their brief show of life in South Davis. There was a little talk of "unilateral neglect," talk that Rachel was ignoring one side of her body as in some of the case histories I'd read, but soon it became clear that the hand and arm were simply crippled with spastic paralysis, as was the right side of her torso and her right leg and foot. Hemiparesis refers to paralysis on one half of the body (as opposed to paraplegis, which is paralysis of either upper or lower limbs). Rachel would be one of the very few brain injured who have physical as well as mental deficits.

Her paralysis, particularly of the right arm and hand, had an uncanny significance for me. My mother, who'd contracted polio at the age of thirty-three, was quadriplegic. Only her left arm, from elbow through to hand, was able to function. Her right arm and hand were completely paralyzed, as were both her legs. Of all my mother's disabilities, I always thought the most tragic was the loss of her right hand. She wrote painstakingly with her left hand, developing a shaky but legible backhanded script, but the day-to-day activities—dressing, eating, cooking, not to mention maneuvering herself from her bed to wheelchair to toilet—were immeasurably more difficult without the use of her right arm and hand. Thus, I knew only too well about infirmity. Throughout Rachel's recovery, the image of my mother's right hand would come to me: ageless, smooth, and perfectly dormant, lying on her lap, the fingers elegantly curved like the stylized fingers of a Sienese Madonna. Would that be Rachel's hand? In fact, it would.

TWO IMPORTANT THINGS were put into operation in the first few weeks of Rachel's rehab at the University hospital. The first was no more diapers. "The worst thing you can do is diaper a brain-injured patient," pronounced Dr. Frank. "It makes them incontinent." The alternative to incontinence, for Dr. Frank, was catheterization. It struck me as a brutal alternative.

Though I have no hard medical proof, I could swear that the catheter contributed to Rachel's severely spastic bladder months down the line. As soon as Rachel showed signs of being able to exercise some bladder control, the catheter would be removed, I was assured. I still didn't get it. How was she supposed to give such a sign with a catheter continually relieving her?

The second goal, as initiated by Sandra, was the removal of her tracheostomy apparatus. This took a few weeks to achieve. Chiefly through Sandra's hard work with Rachel, breathing and blowing, the day came when the trach (not the trachea, of course, but the apparatus connected to it) would be taken out and Rachel would be able to breathe on her own. We were beside ourselves with excitement. Removal of the trach meant Rachel would begin to talk again—maybe. Removal of the trach meant that the g-tube would soon follow and I'd be able to bring her little treats from home—maybe. Removal of the trach would mean she was one step closer to being rehabilitated. I wouldn't have missed the removal of the trach for the world, though I could have done without witnessing it.

The doctor, a young resident with immense self-assurance, raced into her room the morning of the trach removal. He told me he was here to remove the trach, and he was obviously in a hurry to do it. "Terrific," I said. "Should I leave the room?"

"Nah," he said. "There's nothing to it." Then he asked me to hold her arms down.

"I'm lousy with trach stuff," I warned him.

"I've done about two hundred of these," he said, somewhat defensively. "Just hold her arms down." With that he yanked the trach apparatus out of her neck and a thick spurt of blood—I'm talking a *lot* of blood, as in a police drama—shot up at us. At which point, the self-assured resident panicked.

"WHERE'S THE BLAH BLAH BLAH?" he shouted at me. I had no idea what he was talking about. "WHY ISN'T THIS GODDAMN ROOM SET UP PROPERLY?" he shouted, pulling out drawer after drawer while keeping pressure on Rachel's neck.

"NURSE!" I yelled down the hall, and mercifully one came, just as the doctor was attaching some kind of dressing to Rachel's trach incision.

To his credit, this resident sought me out a few days later to apologize. "I didn't have the best bedside manner," he said ruefully. He didn't, and it was very nice of him to say so.

Almost immediately, though, Rachel did well without the trach. "Breathing on her own like a trooper," said Pamela, her great full-time nurse. Pamela had as much faith in Rachel's recovery as I had; she would report each day's or night's triumphs to me if I happened not to catch them first-hand. Pamela, the mother of two girls, told me once, "If it were my daughter, I'd be right there in bed with her, like you are, every day, until she got out of this godforsaken place." Rachel loved Pamela. Her eyes lit up when Pamela came to take her for a bath or a walk or even to check her catheter bag.

In the small speech therapy room, consisting of a table, two chairs, and a shelf full of games, Sandra continued to work on Rachel's breathing. Setting a tiny feather on the table between them, one afternoon, Sandra invited Rachel to blow. Sandra blew first. The feather spun and lifted. To encourage Rachel's lips into the oval, blowing position, Sandra gently squeezed her cheeks. *Fhhhhh, fhhhhh*, Sandra blew. "Come on, Rachel, look at the feather."

Then, incredibly, Rachel produced a faint rush of breath and made the feather flutter. She grinned, looking, for a moment, like the old Rachel. Though I had been insistent that Rachel understood us, I had no proof until she made that feather flutter and then smiled—either at her own success or (more likely) at the silliness of the act itself. But either way, I figured, it was in response to a real event in the real world.

"She made a feather flutter?" asked Margot that night, long distance.

"Just a little. She blew."

"You mean Sandra told her to blow and she blew?"

"Exactly. And then she smiled, kind of mischievously."

"That even sounds like Rache—she *would* see the humor in blowing a wacky feather. That's great news!"

"I know, I know."

"Then what happened?"

"Then she fell asleep."

During this wordless period, when we were graced with only a few precious smiles, Rachel mainly slept. Like a narcoleptic, she would doze off anywhere, in transit to or from the patient lounge or in a room full of visitors or while the doctor was trying to get her to respond to something; but most critically, in the middle of therapies—"Rachel! Rachel! Wake up!" Sandra or Molly or Wendy would say—and I would say it too, because I worried that if she didn't seem to be benefiting from the three hours of therapy a day, insurance might cut out.

I hired a cranio-sacral massage therapist to work on her head and neck, hoping this would encourage alertness. The massage therapist, a tall, kindly woman who lowered the lights, worked on Rachel's cranium for over an hour while I hovered in the doorway. But whatever she did seemed to put Rachel into an even more restful sleep. When we flipped the lights on, her eyes were resolutely closed.

The massage therapist shook her head sadly. "I'm getting from her that she's very tired," she told me.

"What do you mean *you're getting from her*?" I asked.

"Her body is telling me." The therapist had the good grace to blush a little.

"Hmmm" is all I said as I handed her a check. And the therapist made her way to the elevator with her large floral satchel, probably thinking it was a shame that Rachel had been awarded a bitch-mom in this lifetime.

All brain injury patients sleep a lot—I had read this. It's the way the brain heals itself. But for me, the difference between sleep and coma was a little too close for comfort. The sleeping seemed counterproductive, as if we were regressing into the critical coma, and I was worried sick. It would have helped if Dr. Frank had allowed me to attend the weekly team meetings—that is to say, it would have helped *me*. But Dr. Frank was the only doctor in rehab who did not allow family to attend these meetings—and thus, despite my reading of complex brain injury literature (which I puzzled over like a student) and my constant observation of Rachel, I was often in the dark about her formal assessments. After these meetings, I was given a very brief summary by the social worker. Things like "Rachel is doing well without the trach," or "She falls asleep during PT." Duh.

About matters directly related to Rachel's care, I was quite aggressive, but I assumed a passive-resistant attitude when it came to myself. If they wanted to treat me like the moronic, misguided, pain-in-the-ass mom, I could take it. I would not become angry about *that*. That was my position. But why did they—not all of them, not even most of them, but "they" nonetheless—treat me like a moronic, misguided, pain-in-the-ass mom? Because I was reading up on brain injury? Because I was so obviously not docile? Because I was overvigilant? Because I was hopeful?

Now, from a distance of five years, I think it was the latter. Because Rachel's injury was so severe and because I was the mother who refused to accept "reality." What to do with such a person but wish she'd go away?

And so I was given those insulting summaries instead of any real information. My observations were not solicited, and, really, wasn't I the best source of information they had? Because who else studied Rachel as minutely as I did? In retrospect, I can see that they'd given up—they were simply going through the motions of rehab, confident that the outcome would be pretty dismal no matter what.

I did allow myself one minor protest. I told the social worker to tell Dr. Frank to call me either Karen or Dr. Brennan, that I was simply not a Mrs. Anyone. The social worker said she'd report my "concern." After that, the doctor called me nothing. "Hey!" she said once when she passed me in the hall, "I've been looking for you."

It's November and chilly. I sit in Rachel's room and read student stories. In their margins, I pencil comments: *More detail! Watch point of view! This made me laugh! Effective scene!* Rachel is elevated in her bed, awake, then asleep, then awake. I put my pile of papers aside and go to her. I tuck her down comforter under her chin, I kiss her forehead. Her eyes light up. She smiles.

Her eyes light up. She smiles. But still no mouthing of words, no sounds at all.

6

TIM RETURNED FROM his trip to Steamboat Springs after Rache had her trach removed. He brought vitamin E gel-caps to the hospital when he visited, and he'd break them open, rubbing the amber gel onto her tracheostomy scar. It was supposed to be good for healing scars, he said, and Pamela agreed.

But Tim had gotten a job, and he couldn't spend as much time at the hospital as he used to. I felt him withdrawing from Rachel emotionally. He'd gone to Steamboat Springs for his court date, and thanks to my letter, got off with a $250 fine and a vague pledge to do community service. My letter, a master-piece of persuasion, had passionately insisted that the family was not blaming Tim for the accident; continued with a list of Tim's virtues, his remorse paramount among them; and wound up by reaffirming his commitment to Rachel's recovery, his welcome assistance in her rehabilitation.

Tim was already complaining about the fine. I thought of The Predator—would Tim's community service be in a nursing home for the brain injured?

To my great disappointment, he was unable to contact the witness who was to testify on his behalf. I was very anxious to hear what had happened from her point of view. The Steamboat Springs police had told me the story from *their* point of view: that Tim was high, that he'd been driving recklessly, that there were no red telephone company cones in the road and, even, that they'd spoken to the witness, who would confirm what they said. But they didn't have her name, mysteriously, and now Tim couldn't find her. It was not the first thing on my mind, but as the months went on, I felt a need to know exactly what had happened. I felt it was my responsibility to Rachel, even though it was fairly clear that we'd be getting no insurance money from anyone—no "deep pockets," as the attorneys crassly put it, only the shallow, indeed, empty pocket of Tim, who wasn't insured for the motorcycle anyway.

Tim was withdrawing. I suppose it was inevitable that he would, sooner or later. Rachel had "come to," and it was becoming clear that she was not the savvy, worldly-wise girl he'd fallen in love with. She was, instead, a sweet infant who couldn't talk. But he was living at my house, and it was difficult to come home from the hospital one night to discover that he was entertaining one of his female co-workers, one whose name, incredibly, was Rachel. After meeting her, I remember looking at the black-and-white tiles of my kitchen floor and having the sensation that they were shifting under my feet. This Rachel had been sitting on his bed, very comfortably, a lovely young woman with sandy-colored hair who smiled up at me cordially. Upstairs, in the kitchen, the floor seemed to move under my feet. Was this the precursor to a stroke? But I didn't have the luxury to indulge that particular fantasy for long.

Nora and Ron, Tim's parents, drove to Salt Lake laden with gifts for Rachel—little artificial flower arrangements and stuffed animals for her room. And cards, lots of cards, from their neighbors and church group, cards embossed with flowers and teddy bears and signed with love. I could hardly bear it.

Outside the patient lounge, on a hill covered with fading grass and a few brown leaves, Nora and I had a talk. Tim cares for Rachel and he always will, Nora assured me, but he has to get on with his life. He has accepted the fact that things will never be what they were. Oh yeah? I wanted to say. Well, *I* certainly hadn't accepted such a fact.

I was almost happy when Rachel bit Tim's thumb, hard, a few days later. "She drew blood!" said Tim, clearly upset.

RACHEL HAS DEVELOPED a new habit. When she sees me, she grabs my hand and kisses it. Today, on our way back from PT, I badger her: "Do you know who I am, Rache? Do you?" I say. She looks distressed, but I keep it up: "Say yes, Rache, just say yes." And finally, astoundingly, she does. "*Yes*." I have to strain to hear the actual sound, but her mouth forms the word perfectly.

———

IT IS EARLY NOVEMBER, which makes this first word utterance over three months post-accident. I hug and kiss her and she smiles. "One more time, Rache, say yes." "*Yes*." "So does that mean you know me?" "*Yes*." Big smile. "Do you want a doo-doo sandwich for lunch?" Bigger smile. Then, "*No*." She hears! She understands! She speaks! I rush to the nurses station and report our wonderful news. But, since Pamela's not on duty, I get only polite curiosity. Of course, she refuses to perform for anyone else, just like a baby. Rachel has got hold of my hand and is kissing it.

It was exactly like having a baby again. Each day, a new feat. My main mood was elation the last half of that November. I cooed; I bragged. I was the obnoxious mother of a one-year-old: "She said yes! She said no! She kissed! She laughed!" The laughter happened one afternoon on the phone with Geoff. He sang her a song that he and Rache used to make fun of: *You've got to be a special lady and a very exciting girl / You've got to be sitting on top of the world / Just sitting on top of the world.* Then, with the phone cradled between the pillow and her neck, she laughed. She cracked up, throwing her head back on the pillow, shoulders shaking. She laughed soundlessly and I cried.

But when the most dramatic feat of all occurred, I wasn't around. I was teaching my creative writing class, and our friend Jackie was by her bedside, holding forth. Jackie talks a lot under normal circumstances, but with Rachel she went into high gear. She was chatting away when Rachel suddenly interrupted her. "I want my mom," she whispered so faintly that Jackie thought for a moment that she'd imagined it (I tease Jackie and say it was in desperation that Rachel spoke her first sentence). "What did you say?" she asked Rachel. And so Rachel said it again.

This was on November 16, four months post-accident. Jackie called the English Department immediately and dispatched someone to get me from class with the unbelievable news. We had been workshopping a mother-daughter story, haggling over a phrase. Lately, I had taken to looking at my students, especially the twenty-something women, with a combination of awe and envy. It struck me as a kind of miracle that they had survived this far; that they sat in my classroom turning in stories, as now, which pondered the complexities of the mother-daughter relationship; that they constructed metaphors of beauty and precision as blithely as they tossed their shiny, young heads. In another scenario, Rachel could have been among them. Sometimes I'd pretend she was sitting in the back row, puzzling over a sentence or a word choice, oblivious to me, absorbed, as were these students, in the privacy of reflection.

"There are times when," I might have been saying, "the most artless phrase is the truest . . . "

When I looked up, Janet, the undergraduate secretary, was tapping at the plate-glass door with the news: A sentence! A sentence that made sense! "Gotta go," I told the class, who beamed at me, catching my excitement. When I reached the hospital, our friends, Srinivas and Tom, were crouched beside Rachel's wheelchair, the better to hear her faint but unmistakable voice. She spoke in a tiny whisper, but it was clearly talking, it was clearly sensible: clear, beautiful, lovely words.

Spotting me, she was almost querulous. Grabbing my arm,

she whispered, "Where were you?" "Oh Rache!" I kept saying. "Oh Mom," she said back. Each string of words seemed to wear her out. Her face had taken on a beaten, sorrowful look. "I love you," I said. "I love you," she said back. Her voice was fading—I found myself lip-reading in desperation. Then she closed her eyes; when she opened them, minutes later, she glanced around the room without much curiosity.

Later, after I tucked her in, I got down on my knees in front of Rachel's Guadalupe picture and said, *Thanks, but don't stop here, please.*

As the weeks went on, in between long bouts of drowsiness, Rachel would talk constantly. She was a bit disarthric— that is, her speech was slow, slurred, and still whispered, and certain consonants were tricky. She called Pamela "Bamela," for example—and we loved that.

The pre-injury Rachel was, like the rest of her siblings, nothing if not ironic. It was the mainstay of her pre-injury personality, an outrageous and wacky sense of humor. Take the way she and Tim met, for example: He was in a bar in Aspen, Colorado, when Rachel breezed in, caught his eye, and settled herself next to him on a bar stool. Silence prevailed. They both looked straight ahead, she seemingly indifferent to his presence. Then she turned to him and said: "What's with the hair?" A little annoyed, Tim excused himself and went to the rest room. When he returned, she was still sitting there, a bemused expression on her face. "So," she said after he sat down again, "do you have an opinion about the Ebola virus?" After that, he "got" her and they had a great time.

However, I had read in the literature that irony was very difficult for brain injured patients. Irony is a higher brain function, requiring two levels of thought and the wit to discriminate between them—to mark the absurdity or the incongruity in both language and life. brain injured patients are very concrete, I had read. They are literal-minded, not agile enough to switch gears. I had resigned myself to this. In fact, one day in physical therapy, Molly, praising Rachel for her hard work that session, said, "Rache, you are such a little animal." I panicked. "Don't say that," I told Molly. "She'll think she *is* an animal." Molly, to her credit, rolled her eyes.

After all, I *did* have some clues that Rachel's humor was intact. She had laughed at Geoff's song, thereby acknowledging an old-time joke between them. And the doo-doo sandwich got a big smile. But it wasn't until the day when a downtrodden-looking hospital worker was mopping the floor of Rachel's room that her irony was unmistakable. In her tiny whisper, by way of a thank you, she told him, "You rock my world . . . as small as it is."

After that, she was unstoppable. Everyone rocked her small world and everyone was subject to a joke. Dr. Frank she referred to, sardonically, as her "medic" and Dr. Peterson was a "hotty." Her therapists all became "Girlfriend," and me she called a variety of names, "Matcha," "Matcha Bean," "Girlfriend Jones," the silliest of which was "Casserole," a joke name my kids had taken to calling me after I told them the story of how their dad's mother, having imbibed a bit too much bourbon one night, introduced me to a room full of guests as "Casserole" instead of Karen. "Casserole," Rachel would say, "I love you." And now she called Pamela "Bamela" on purpose.

Her antics recalled the bizarre results of her sixth-grade vocational test. Recommendations for Rachel's career had

been as follows: *stand-up comic, ventriloquist, magician.*
"Whatever happened to *nurse?*" asked John.

Though she seemed now to be fulfilling her fate as some kind of performer, not everyone saw her humor as humor. To some, this was the brain injury, this was "disinhibition," a pathological lack of inhibition caused by damage to the right frontal lobe. Well, she was disinhibited; but rather than manic swearing or masturbating—the usual symptoms of disinhibition—Rachel was simply a wise guy. "I'll take that any day," I told Dr. Frank. Plus it proved, didn't it, that she was in there somewhere, the same old Rachel?

It's true that, unlike her former self, Rachel no longer had a great sense of audience. She treated everyone as if they were members of our screwball family. She didn't (doesn't often) read people well. She kissed the hands of the unaffectionate and cracked jokes with the humorless. For this latter group, Rachel's oddball humor was especially upsetting. They didn't get it, and so it struck them as strange, in the same way that brain injury behaviors are apt to be strange. This was especially frustrating for me. I wanted people—especially the medical staff—to see Rachel's wit as a strength that indicated a better prognosis. Instead, they deemed it an upsetting pathology.

Even Sandra was uncertain when she tested Rachel's vocab skills. Rachel either cracked wise (disinhibition) or, in the case of one test, provided quirky, "nonstandard" comebacks to questions like *Name an article of clothing.* Rachel's answer: *earmuffs.* And when asked to name a red fruit, Rachel said, *Pomegranate.* But how to convince Sandra or anyone that "earmuffs" and "pomegranate" are creative responses, betraying Rachel's refusal to be ordinary? And that this, too, represented her struggle to recover herself?

———

WHAT IS NORMAL? Sooner or later, anyone who is involved with brain injury—and that's a lot of us these days—is confronted with this question. In our culture, we are swamped with intimidating notions of normality. Behaviors, attitudes, social conduct, even emotions are supposed to measure up (or down) to some vague standard. I say "vague" because who really knows? Certainly "normal" refers more to culture than to nature, more to societal values than to what is innately human. What is considered normal behavior for a Maori tribesman, for example, would be considered pathological behavior for a stockbroker. And so on. Too often, the principle of normality seems predicated on the average. The average Joe or Jane or Rachel wouldn't pick up a guy in a bar by asking his opinion of the Ebola virus. I'm just thinking out loud here. My daughter is most assuredly not normal. Was she ever normal? Was I? When does the "not" become "ab"?

What brain injury teaches us is that brain injuries are as individual as people. Neurologically speaking, we each have billions of brain cells which, as a result of environment, education, and experience, not to mention DNA, develop in idiosyncratic ways. I'm trying to think of a metaphor. Something little and active. Ants won't do; they're too ruly. The brain is anything but ruly. It is associative, electrical; it works like a good conversation, sparking this or that topic and synthesizing information, feelings, genetic predispositions, and memory. There are billions of ways a brain can develop. So and so is good at math; so and so has a photographic memory; so and so is predisposed to depression. Which explains why brain injuries are as individual as people.

In Rachel's case, damage to her left frontal lobe did not produce severe aphasia. Was this because the neuronal clusters in that knot of language—the Broca Wart—were richly developed due to her second-language ability? Because she'd been a reader and was a college graduate? Because, in that area, she could afford to lose a few brain cells?

On the other hand, was she vulnerable to disinhibition since she'd had so little inhibition to begin with? Or is what they call "disinhibition" just the old Rachel with a few tweaks? Or just the old Rachel period?

These are the matters I mull over late at night, in the darkness of my small Third Avenue bedroom, a cold November moon shining through the window and making my fingers look green. Aren't we all brain damaged in some way? Tomorrow I will put Rachel in her furry leopard hat and take her for a long walk.

THANKSGIVING'S COMING and the g-tube is still in. No real food yet. Because of her low weight, Dr. Frank is reluctant to take her off her regulated nutrients. We've all observed that she just doesn't seem hungry. I nibble a Milky Way in front of her, hoping to get her mouth watering, but she's not so interested in her former pleasures. She *is* interested in seeing Margot, Steve, and the kids, who will spend the holiday with us. And John, ex-husband number 2, will take a six-week leave of absence from his attorney's job to stay with me.

I am impatient for everyone's arrival. I spruce up the house, buy fresh flowers, remove several layers of dust from the tops of everything with an old T-shirt, and plan the Thanksgiving feast in the same spirit I always have at this time of year—half-joyous and half-frantic. In the throes of late autumn, Salt Lake has a weary, dreamy quality; the leaves are in brown piles in front of my house and the air is sharp and fragrant with wood smoke from my neighbors' chimneys.

John arrives first, having driven eight hundred miles from Tucson in our ancient Honda, which now sports two Frisbee-sized dents on the driver's side. Perhaps this is why he was pulled over in southern Utah by a cop who was convinced that John was, if not a drug dealer, at least a drug imbiber. John, with his post-divorce hair, his earring (now a long silver feather he'd purchased on the Navajo reservation), was perversely delighted with his adventure. "Why didn't you tell him you're an attorney?" I wonder. John grins. "Eventually I did. I wanted to wait and see if he did an illegal search."

Whatever our failings as marriage partners, John and I are simpatico in the domestic sphere. Without a word, we began chopping veggies for a stir-fry, part of which we take to Rachel that evening. Later, we watch episodes of *Law and Order* on my queen-sized bed. It's a tremendous comfort to have him there, someone to share the dailiness of this nightmare for more than a long weekend. And though real laughs are hard to come by these days, John's droll sense of humor always cheers me up. I feel a huge release of tension; I actually begin sleeping through the night.

Rachel is delighted to see John. She holds his hand and kisses it. "Oh Johnny," she says over and over. "You rock my world as small as it is." (She would say this for years, to anyone, at the slightest provocation—her first post-accident joke having taken, perhaps, an unfortunate stronghold.) Then:

"Your hair is so long!" She fingers a strand of it wonderingly. Well now, I think, watching the two of them. I'm off the hook for a minute. Maybe I'll go buy a turkey.

Margot and the kids will arrive the next day, the day before Thanksgiving, and Steve will come on the players' plane on Thanksgiving Day. It is occasions like these that allow me to pretend we are normal family, intact and healthy, almost invulnerable. I buy turkey, fixings, and fresh flowers like a regular mom, all the while studying the other regular moms in the grocery store aisles and wondering just how regular any of us really are.

Early Thanksgiving morning, while John does Rachel duty, Margot and I cook. We stuff, chop, melt, and rolling pin for hours, the kids playing happily in the background. On the stereo a Beethoven string quartet provides the perfect accompaniment to our industry, and some combination of cello, violin, and roasting turkey puts me into near-ecstasy. One-year-old Maddy sits on my bed amid four or five pillows solemnly turning the pages of a *New Yorker*; Nick dances to the Beethoven. Someone should draw all of us, right this minute, I think, thinking, too, how precarious it all is, how absolutely fragile.

At noon, with the help of Srinivas and Ranjii, my Utah family, we haul carloads of turkey and stuffing and veggies and pies (and even wine, which was probably forbidden) and plates, silverware, cloth napkins, and wineglasses to the rehab patient lounge. There we move two or three of the rectangular Formica tables together, cover them with a big red-and-white-checked linen cloth, set it with my white plates, and even manage an autumnal bouquet and candles for a centerpiece. Very elegant. We push Rachel to the head of the table in her chair, where she falls asleep almost immediately; when she "comes to," she is so cranky (overwhelmed?) that I have to put her to bed.

The patient lounge becomes suddenly ordinary, itself again, with unattractive polyester curtains over the smudged windows and urine-colored fluorescent lights and grimy vinyl tiles on the floor. And the table looks silly, even a little pathetic. We eat with dutiful Thanksgiving gusto, but it is a lackluster occasion without Rachel.

Later that night, a redemption: Rache and John and I are watching the Bulls-Jazz game in the hospital room when the commentator interrupts his play-by-play to say that Steve Kerr has asked him to send love and best wishes to his sister-in-law Rachel Brennan, who is recovering from a motorcycle accident at the University of Utah hospital. "Hey, Rache, did you hear that? You're famous!" "You mean the Bulls—me—Stevie—wow!"

THE LOATHSOME G-TUBE is gone, its removal much less traumatic than the trach removal, with just a little tug. Rachel can now eat real food. I bring her brie, her favorite, and lots of chocolate, juice smoothies, homemade cookies, chicken soup. But Rachel is afraid to swallow. She is afraid to eat.

I make it a point to come every mealtime, in between classes, to feed her her dinner at the community meal served in the patient lounge. Still terror. Word comes to me via the social worker that the doctor thinks I might be traumatizing her. Issues of mothers and food? We never had any. But okay, then, I do not come at mealtimes—I lurk in the hall outside the patient lounge, tearing off my nails while Wendy tries to feed Rachel. No luck. It is speculated that she has some spasticity in her throat, that the trach scar is causing her discomfort, that she may have a swallowing disorder, common in head injury and stroke victims.

In about a week, Sandra breaks through, painstakingly training her to swallow until she loses her fear. There is still some difficulty with liquids, but we're on our way. Wendy is working on manners since Rachel's tendency is to eat with her hand and dribble food down the front of her shirt. Well, she's really hungry.

Then there's the evening we're seated at a long table of rehab diners. An elderly stroke victim is playing the piano, cocktail music from the '30s. When he joins us at the table, he speaks earnest and quite reasonable-sounding gibberish. His pretty wife is seated there too, bearing up. The others are mainly silent, intent on their food, uncommunicative. Rachel is looking around expectantly, but no one is inclined to talk except the man who makes no sense. Rachel gives him a superior look, then announces, "I really have to take a dump." Well, she really has to take a dump.

Later in the week, Rachel is "written up" by her night nurse for abusive language. She continually has the urge to go to the bathroom, despite the catheter. When the catheter is removed, she is able, hurrah!, to pee in the pot. But the urge persists. Every ten minutes, she has to pee and she's wearing out the nurses, who have to lift her onto the portable potty. And then, most of the time, she is unable to go. So the rule has become no peeing for at least twenty minutes. Rachel cannot adhere to this rule. She pleads with the nurses and is refused. Thus, the abusive language.

But I have to wonder at this nurse who writes her up.

Foul language is common in brain injury cases—and my sweet, polite daughter is no exception.

Now that she's fully awake (though still prone to drowsiness) and talking and without catheter, trach, and g-tube, Dr. Frank schedules an MRI. This will be the first one since that awful blood-spot-on-the-brain one in Denver. She is chatting away happily, awake for once, as John and I wheel her down the long hospital corridors. In the MRI cylinder she can't lie still. The technicians try again and again. On the fourth try, after pleading with her to hold still, they pull Rachel out of the cylinder.

"What's wrong, Rachel?" a nice white-coated technician asks her. "Why are you moving around so much?"

Rachel's response: "I always try to sit up when I'm in new places."

"Okay," the technician tells me, "we'll have to sedate her."

"No," I say.

"No?" he says.

"No," I say, and I wheel her back to her room.

Of course, this annoys Dr. Frank, who assures me that Rachel can safely undergo anesthesia. But in the back of my mind is a story I heard when Rachel was in South Davis: A previously comatose boy went home for a weekend and drank one beer, which sent him back into a weeklong coma. How much more dangerous would anesthesia be? Of course, what do I know? I'm flying by the seat of my pants, by hunches and stories rather than by facts.

In a week I have another run-in with the doctor. Rachel has developed a syndrome in her right arm called reflexive sympathetic dystrophy, commonly referred to as RSD. The arm has turned purple-ish and hurts. This is a complicated neurological syndrome which involves a screwup of messages between the sympathetic and parasympathetic nervous systems, and it's important that it's caught early. Otherwise the affected limb could atrophy.

To her credit, Dr. Frank is right on top of this. She prescribes a drug combo which includes the antidepressant Elavil. The morning after her first dose, Rachel's pupils are dilated, and she seems as if she's in a semi-stupor. All day, she is zonked, not so much sleepy as out of it, zombie-ish. No conversation and, for the first time, it seems she's having difficulty recognizing people, including me. That night I spend hours poring through my brain injury books and discover that there are several effective ways to treat RSD, the Elavil cocktail only one among them. The next day I rise at six and station myself by Rachel's door before seven so I can catch the nurse with the med tray.

"She's not taking that," I say.

"Doctor's orders," says the nurse brightly.

"Sorry," I say, blocking her passage. "Have the doctor call me."

The doctor telephones that afternoon, more than a little peeved. When I explain my position, she agrees to try her on something called Varopomil. Varopomil is a beta-blocker and requires frequent monitoring of the liver, but trying it is preferable to Rachel's regressing to a zombie state.

I'm getting weary of this battle. It's snowing, and the big, soft flakes of Utah fill Rachel's window as in a TV movie of snow. On the way home, at ten or so, I skid on a steep hill and my heart lurches along with the car.

7

I only know myself as a human entity; the scene, so to speak, of thoughts and affections; and am sensible of a certain doubleness by which I can stand as remote from myself as from another. However intense my experience, I am conscious of the presence and criticism of a part of me, which, as it were, is not a part of me, but spectator, sharing no experience, but taking note of it: and that is no more I than it is you.
— HENRY DAVID THOREAU, "Solitude," *Walden*

WHY DO THE DOCTORS continue to be unimpressed with Rachel's progress? This is why: As witty and verbal as she is showing herself to be, a crippling disability is revealing itself: She has absolutely no short-term memory. From minute to minute, even second to second, she can't retain what's said to her, what she did, whom she spoke to. Nor does she know, despite continual cues and reminders and drills, where she is or what happened to her. She knows her family and her friends—she always recognizes the important people in her life. She remembers most of her past, with a few notable gaps: Italy, where she'd spent the summer is a blank to her, as is her last year of college, including her graduation. "Did I graduate from college?" is one of her persistent, anxious questions, to which we give an answer again and again, complete with GPA; but she can't seem to hold the answer in her mind. Short-term memory.

The doctors are referring to this notable problem as PTA, post-traumatic amnesia, which occurs commonly after trauma to the brain. PTA, however, is supposed to clear up after a few weeks. Rachel's doesn't. There's a chilling adage which is part of the brain injury literature: the longer the PTA, the worse the prognosis. I am told this in no uncertain terms by Dr. Antonini, one of the physiatrists on call over the weekend.

I catch Dr. Antonini in the patient lounge on Saturday morning. He seems preoccupied; when he sees me, he picks up a magazine and turns his back. Nevertheless, I persist.

"Dr. Antonini," I say. "I'd like to ask you a few questions about Rachel."

"Okay," he says nervously, almost defensively, "but I can't give you a prognosis. No one can predict the outcome of an injury as severe as Rachel's."

"I understand that. But I have a few specific questions and concerns I'd like to run by you."

And then—had he even heard me?—he blurts out the following: "With a PTA as prolonged as Rachel's, the prognosis for recovery is very poor."

I forget my specific questions. I'm wondering instead: Why did the doctor give a prognosis when he said he couldn't give one? When I get home that day, I fling myself on my bed. My heart is skipping beats and I count them, one, two, five. Then I get down on my knees to Guadalupe—by this time, I have a picture of her in every room. *Help us through this*, I pray. *Just please please please help us through this.* By the end of the weekend I feel marginally better.

THERE ARE TIMES when I feel that I am on the outside looking in at my life, and that the life I look at has shrunk to the size of a dime somewhere at a football-field length away from me—tiny, colorless, giving off a hard glint. I'm sure this is what the shrinks call disassociation, a condition which is the consequence of a tragedy too unbearable to exist within.

But I'm thinking also about what Thoreau says about *doubleness*—having a consciousness that observes as well as one that is in the action. Thoreau's idea of doubleness—standing "remote from myself," as he puts it—is closer to the trick I've cultivated through the years, a writer's doubleness: a way of looking at my life as an unfolding story, of framing my experience for the sake of art. At Denver, I was struck, for example, by the perfect narrative shape of that family gathering, like a novel that worked backward from its "tragedy" to separate narrative strands: births, marriages, divorces. My observer self is the one who supplies the inverted commas, who makes the cool transfer from life to art. My other self rushes around, weeps, tears off my fingernails, while over my shoulder the observer is gathering material: *The mother is weeping, a tear falls onto her white linen shirt, leaving a gray-ish blot; the mother is getting hotheaded or befuddled or edgy. Now the mother marches down the hospital corridor conscious of her rubber-soled platforms making dull thuds on the floor.*

That other self dogged me with special vehemence during the crisis part of this real-life story, taking notes, making callous ironic judgments, even, and most perversely, making me ashamed of my habits of observation, as if the writer in me were more powerful than the person.

For example: One day a social worker visits the mother in the daughter's room. She has with her several forms. She asks the mother kindly if she would like to apply for guardianship of Rachel. The mother says no, that she would rather wait and see if that will be necessary. The social worker assures her this will be necessary. The mother stubbornly refuses to apply for guardianship. The social worker then flips to another form and asks if the mother has given any consideration to where Rachel will go after acute rehabilitation. The mother says that after acute rehabilitation, Rachel will come home with her. The social worker tells the mother gently, kindly, that this would be inadvisable, that she will help the mother select a good nursing home. Nevertheless, the mother insists that she will take her daughter home. She tells the social worker she would take her daughter home with a trach and a catheter and a g-tube, if necessary. She tells the social worker there are no circumstances under which she will not take her daughter home. It is hardly surprising, therefore, that the social worker will eventually evaluate "the mother" as a "liability" to "the daughter."

These are the words she will write in Rachel's file: "The mother's unrealistic expectations are interfering with the daughter's recovery." *Is it possible that the mother's denial is so fierce that even the word of a medical professional will not bring her to her senses?*

Each evening, the mother and the ex-husband trudge out

to the car in the snow, drive home down the increasingly slippery hill and, once inside the cozy but increasingly filthy house, lie on the bed and watch *Law and Order*. This is what I yearn for, Law and Order in my life: a set of rules to follow or, more pertinently, a catastrophe, a trial, justice. "Nothing about this is really *fair*," I tell John. "Life's not fair," he says, and we both grin because, in the past, that had been my line.

In the mornings, Dr. Frank makes her rounds. When she gets to Rachel's room she has a routine. She says, "Where are you, Rachel?" And Rachel looks out the window for a clue. Brick wall, blue sky. Tucson? Colorado? New York? Every morning Rachel has no idea where she is.

The second question is, "What's my name, Rachel?"

Rachel hems and haws. "Well, Girlfriend," she says, "fuck if I know."

This answer does not amuse her doctor. "Rachel," she continues, "what month is it?"

"Hmmm," says Rachel. "March?"

"And the year?" 1991? 1994? 1988? She has no idea.

She never has any idea. Today, five years post-injury, Rachel still has trouble with the date and—I suppose this logically follows—with her age. My question: Is this post-traumatic amnesia or a short-term memory deficit? No one ever attempts to answer me.

Meawhile, Rachel's sleeping is interfering with the therapy. If she doesn't stay awake, therapy becomes nonproductive. If therapy is nonproductive, insurance won't pay. If insurance won't pay, she'll be shunted to a nursing home like South Davis. There must be some way, I insist, of getting her out of drowse stage and there is.

One day Rachel is given what must have been a hefty

dose of Dexedrine. When I come in from teaching at supper-time, she is at the nurse's station, strapped to her chair, trying to manipulate a computer with her one good hand. She is talking a blue streak, swearing intermittently but good-naturedly, pounding the computer, gobbling chocolate chip cookies, laughing. General hilarity prevails around the nurses station, and at the center is Rachel. Dr. Peterson is scribbling notes on charts, blushing wildly, while Rachel holds forth at his expense. "He's *such* a hotty," she says.

Then, amazingly, she begins to recite the Gettysburg address. On and on she goes and when she gets to *Now we are engaged in a great civil war*, she puts up her arm, Lincoln-like. We're all laughing, but mixed with my laughter is pure aston-ishment. She gives me a sidelong glance: "Mr. Wait. Sixth-grade social studies. We got extra credit if we memorized it."

After the Gettysburg, she moves to a rap song called "Fly Girl" and recites the whole thing. The last lines go: *You're not the prettiest thing girl / but that's ok / your painted-on jeans make you fresh anyway.*

"Geez," said a friend when I reported these bizarre feats, "that's the whole of American history in a nutshell."

After that, the Dexedrine was deep-sixed.

THE REAL WORLD is crackling with Christmas. Lights dazzle from the huge pine trees of Salt Lake; sleighs full of fake presents and gaudy angels with yellow Lucite wings decorate the big front porches and snowy yards. I see my neighbor negotiate her icy walk, laden with gifts. It all has little effect on me. I do not get into the spirit. I think only of what I could buy for Rachel, as if that would make a difference.

There is a field trip organized by the recreational therapist, and Rachel goes along, me at her side. We ride to the
University museum in the handicapped van. All inhabitants,
except for the few accompanying parents and the rec therapist driver, are in wheelchairs, which get buckled down. The
whole procedure makes Rachel impatient. By comparison,
the other brain injured are docile, well-behaved, but also, I
have to admit, somewhat spaced-out. "Where the fuck are
we going?" Rachel asks many times in her hoarse whisper.

After hauling the group of brain injured out and into the
museum, we discover that only the permanent collection—a
dark array of portraits and turn-of-the-century landscapes—
is available for spectators. Rachel, by this time, is irate. "This
is so stupid!" she's screaming, if you can call it screaming.
"Whose idea was THIS?" She is so mad her right side
spasms; she makes a fist with her left hand and slams it on
the arm of the chair.

In desperation, I push her to the gift shop, where she is
immediately taken with a pair of earrings. This, I would learn
later, is a phenomenon called being "stimulus bound," meaning that brain injured persons are easily, indeed instantaneously, distracted by new stimuli. The earrings are gold with
some kind of blue stone and cost forty dollars. She fingers one
longingly, so I buy them for her. I will later present them to
her on many occasions—Christmas, Valentine's Day, you-
name-it day—and Rachel will always respond with surprise
and delight. "That's kind of mean," says Margot, "but funny."

For Christmas, Chris and Geoff will fly in from San
Francisco, and Tom, Rachel's father, will fly up from Tucson. I
am told that Rachel will be able to come home on Christmas
Eve and spend one night with us. So finally, about a week

before Christmas, I begin getting a little spirit. I buy stockings to fill, and John and I select a tree. I actually make a trip to the mall and fight through the crowds for a few gifts. The idea that Rachel will come home especially thrills me. Once home, I'm convinced, she might orient herself a little better.

But we've entered another weird phase of recovery, this time with something the brain books call "confabulation." "Cinderella smashed all the windows," Rachel announced sadly one morning. "Excuse me?" I said. A few days later, she told me that she had finally figured out where we were— in a plane over Vietnam. There was a war going on. It all made sense to her, she said. "Well . . . maybe," I said.

Rachel was confabulating. Confabulation is one of those brain injury pathologies wherein the brain injured, in extreme confusion, begin to make stuff up. When I wasn't worried about the psychotic "feel" of these confabulations, I have to admit they delighted me. They were bizarrely metaphorical: Weren't Cinderella and her smashed windows a good analogy for Rachel's current situation? And, as in episodes of *M*A*S*H*, wasn't the plane over Vietnam a story that "made sense" out of trauma? And when the nurse reported that, during the range-of-motion exercises with her right arm, Rachel joyfully proclaimed that she was giving birth to a baby, I naturally saw it as a sign of hope. "She's giving birth to herself!" I said, an interpretation that was met with the pity look.

But the confabulations hit high gear the day that Rachel confided to the nurses that Margot was not her real sister. She *knew* this; she'd overheard someone called Fiona tell someone else; but I, her mother, didn't know she knew. She told the nurses they better not tell me. When one of the nurses approached me with this complicated story, she was visibly torn. "You should know that Rachel knows that Margot is not her real sister."

"I beg your pardon?" I said.

The nurse's face was full of concern. "She overheard Fiona tell someone."

"Who is Fiona?" I asked.

"Well, I'm sure I have no idea," said the nurse. "I thought she was a friend."

"Margot is certainly her real sister and we know no Fiona. Rachel is confabulating."

But I couldn't seem to persuade the nurses of this. Rachel had so convinced them of my complicity that, for a few days, they gave me suspicious looks (*now the mother is doing her best to confuse the daughter even more*). But maybe I'm imagining this. Because during the relatively short period of Rachel's confabulations, I felt as though we'd dropped through the looking glass into a strange upside-down world. What was true? What was false? And how the hell did uncertainties about Margot get tangled up in Rachel's topsy-turvy brain? What did it mean? I was always asking that question in those days.

Rachel's most hilarious confabulation came a few days before Christmas when Tom, her father, just off the plane from Tucson, visited Rachel with a woman friend, whose name was Ginny. Rachel knew Ginny from the old days when, for a short time, she'd dated Tom. I knew Ginny very slightly myself, a perky, well-dressed woman with one foot in new age–dom.

"Ginny!" she cried. "How wonderful to see you!" I was

surprised at the enthusiasm—as far as I knew, Rachel hadn't known Ginny very well.

"Nice to see you too, Rachel," said Ginny, somewhat taken aback.

"Oh Ginny!" said Rachel, grabbing Ginny's hand and kissing it ardently. "I'm so very, very glad to see you!"

"Hey, me too Rache!" was Ginny's game response.

Then, a few minutes later, she said it again. "Oh Ginny!" And again.

"We *know* you're glad to see Ginny, honey," I finally said in exasperation.

"It's only that I'm so glad what I heard about you isn't true," said Rachel.

"What did you hear about me?" asked Ginny. I felt I had to intervene. God only knew what was coming next. "Rachel is a little confused these days," I explained. "She's sort of, uh, making stuff up."

"I'm not, I'm not!" said Rachel. "I heard you had"—now Rachel lowered her voice—"passed on." Passed on?

"In fact," Ginny said, lowering her voice, "I did have a near-death experience this fall." Oh *please*, I'm thinking.

But Rachel wouldn't let it alone. "I'm so relieved!" she said, putting her good left hand over her heart. "I'm so glad to see you!" The conversation drifted to other things, but not for long. Soon Rachel interrupted again. "I'm SO glad to see you, Ginny!"

When Tom and Ginny left, I said to Rachel, "I guess you were *really really* glad to see Ginny."

"She's in my prayers every single night," Rachel said solemnly.

deranged. In one especially disturbing photograph, she is wearing a Santa stocking cap askew, slumped into the sofa cushions, her blue eyes as big as saucers and just as vacant.

TONIGHT, FOR THE UMPTEENTH time I put Rachel on the pot, and for the umpteenth time, she couldn't produce anything but a tiny trickle; when I took her off we spotted a real green pea in the pot (it must have been a dinner remnant). "Look, a pea!" I said. Rachel breaks into laughter—she loves nothing better than a good pun. It seems as if the world is conforming to some strange Rachel reality.

RACHEL'S PROPENSITY to repeat herself is called, in brain injury speak, "perseveration." If confabulation is replacing fact with fantasy, concocting wild tales to compensate for a lack of memory, free associating, then perseveration is a failure of imagination, a failure of association, free or otherwise. Perseveration—a word I find especially illuminating, to persevere too much, as I take it—reflects a rigidity on the part of the perseverator. The perseverator can only repeat, and this repetition is like the manic activity of the hamster running around its little track. One can almost feel the glitch in some neuronal loop, the inability to jump off.

Rachel perseverates all the time now. She gets stuck on a series of questions, which I answer over and over. *What happened to me? Where am I? What will happen next? Do I have a boyfriend? What day is it? What year is it?* And as soon as the series has been answered, she begins again. I am estimating her short-term memory to be no more than a minute in length. When I leave her hospital room for five minutes, she cannot remember that I am here.

SOMETIME IN JANUARY, I take Rachel to the doctor at the Moran Eye Clinic at the hospital, and she is fitted with glasses, which at least mask her wayward eyes. The eye doctor is more informative than any doctor has been in our three-and-a-half-month stay at the University hospital. She explains that Rachel's brain-stem injury—that tiny spot on the brain stem—has affected her vision, but that, despite Rachel's deficits, she is "smart." Her eyes have learned to compensate for seeing double; her right eye simply has trained itself to stop seeing.

She also explains Rachel's new laugh—a kind of crazy guffaw that sounds like Horshack on the '70s TV show *Welcome Back, Kotter*. The laugh is characteristic of someone with a brain-stem injury, she tells me. "When will it go away?" Margot asks.

Indeed, Rachel is always laughing. Her laughter echoes down the hospital corridors, *haw haw haw*, gulping in air. "She's not serious about anything," complained one nurse. "It runs in the family," I said, remembering my favorite student evaluation from an ESL class I taught long ago. The evaluator, an earnest Korean student, had written the following: *This teacher should learn to be more serious in the classroom. She should know this is not enjoy class for her life.* "Like mother, like daughter," I told the nurse.

FEBRUARY 2, 1996, is Rachel's release date. She has "plateaued," according to the doctor, and so insurance is going to cut out. I am encouraged, once again, to consider putting her in a nursing home. No way, I told them. The morning of the second, I'm racing around, packing Rachel's stuff, including her giant poster of Lenny Kravitz and her Guadalupe calendar, her boom box, her CDs and tapes, her cards and presents, her paper flowers, family photos, and, last but most cumbersome, a giant banner from a wonderful group of junior high students in Tucson which reads DON'T GIVE UP RACHEL.

I meet with the head of outpatient rehab, a pleasant but somewhat nervous woman with a tight perm who tells me to expect a "regression" when Rachel returns home, since this is common when TBI patients make a change of any sort. I meet with Molly, Sandra, and Wendy, and we all hug. Sue tells me that some patients are special, have special meaning for her, and Rachel is one of those. We are all a little teary.

But I'm hunting for Dr. Frank. I need to know about meds, I need prescriptions, I need advice. I finally find her outside the PT room, and this is when she says, for the first and only time, "Hey! I've been looking for you," carefully avoiding calling me a name.

"Me too," I say. "I'm taking Rachel home."

"Yeah, I know," she says. "But you should know that Rachel has made all the recovery she's going to make. It's six months since the accident."

"Well, we'll see," I say. Luckily, I'd done my homework. TBI survivors can make progress for years after an injury.

As if she's read my mind, Dr. Frank gives me a stony

look. "She'll never be able to live an independent life. The memory." Then, incredibly, she shrugs, taps her metal file with a pen, and rushes down the hall before I can ask her about meds.

It turns out that Pamela has organized Rachel's meds and prescriptions, and she is teary, too, when we hug her good-bye. "We love you, Bamela," I say. "Later, skater," says Rachel, kissing Pamela's freckled hand.

But our day wouldn't have been complete without the obligatory last chat with the social worker. She, too, has nothing encouraging to say.

"It'll only get worse," she says.

"No," I say, "the worst would have been if Rachel had died." She raises an eyebrow and looks at me meaningfully. "Are you saying it would have been *better* if Rachel had died?" I ask her.

"Good luck," she says.

Oh well. We're going home. It's February. Snow covers the valley and the black tree limbs. Rachel is in her wheel-chair, slumped to one side, her glasses askew, her leopard hat plopped on her head. "Where are we going again? Where are we going again?" she whispers. I say, "Home, home, home." She is smiling and ready. So am I. So am I.

8

Where we have lush forests of recall to turn to, [Mr. M.] has only a few gray, dried trees. We move through time as through a landscape, able to see things coming from far away and able to orient ourselves with expectations of what will come next. For him the world does not come naturally from a landscape, but bursts out of a wall of mist.
        —PHILIP J. HILTS, *Memory's Ghost*

ONE WEEKEND IN January of 1996 was sort of a pre-home-coming trial, just the two of us, *sans* the rest of the family. On Saturday, Rachel lay in my queen-sized bed with the covers pulled up to her neck. "Where are we?" she asked. "Katonah? Peach Lake?"

The blinds were up on the window in my tiny, mostly shadowy room, and it was a kind of East Coast–looking day in Salt Lake City: the same pearled, opaque sky, the same bare branches tangling against it. Despite the logic of branches and sky, her lack of orientation upset me. After months of confusion, I thought that at least she *knew* we were in Salt Lake and not New York, didn't she? "Where am I?" she kept asking. I put my arms around her and stroked her forehead. "How old are you, Rachel?" I asked.

"I think I must be in my twenties."

"Yes. And how old were you when we lived in Katonah and Peach Lake?"

"I was young. Three or four."

"Then where are we?"

"I don't know. New York?"

Soon after, she wanted the lights out. She told me she wanted to die. "Why did this happen to me?" she asked, initiating a mantra I came to be only too familiar with. "Why didn't I just die?" And then: "Why didn't God take me?" Her voice seemed even less substantial than usual, barely a fragment of a voice. I had to put my ear near her mouth to hear. Her lovely dark hair tangled on the pillow. She wouldn't let me brush it.

I left her in the dark room that cold January Saturday. I sat in the kitchen outside the bedroom door, and every once in a while, I'd check on her. She was sleeping, finally, and then she slept on and off all day. Every twenty minutes or so I took her to the john. Once a friend stopped by to see her, and when I told Rachel she had a visitor, she said "Please, do I have to see them? I don't want to see them." The friend left. I sat in the kitchen. I took her to the john. When the time came, I put on my pajamas, crawled into bed with her and held her, unnerved—because what was this? Suicidal depression? Psychosis?—through the night. Sunday was the same.

Those disheartening days come vividly to mind this morning of February 2, the day of Rachel's real homecoming. Will Rachel plummet into a severe depression once she comes home? What can I do to prevent it? How can I make a life for her, a recovery for her, possible?

Weeks before she'd asked my friend Meg if I really wanted her to come home. "Of course she wants you to come home," Meg assured her. This conversation, when Meg reported it, made me feel guilty. Because what had I said or done to make Rachel doubt me? Or perhaps (grim comfort) it was projection; perhaps it was Rachel who wasn't sure if she could bear her new life.

Now we are on our way home for good, and Rachel, it seems, is happy enough. In the car, she holds my hand and kisses it while I pull the car one-handed into a space at the curb (we don't have a garage). I hoist her from the chair to the car, then from the car to the chair, schlepping the wheelchair out of the trunk each time. My friend David had built a ramp going up to the front porch and painted it green. He even mixed sand into the paint to prevent slipping during the winter.

I push her up the ramp. She weighs in at a sylphlike 110 pounds. The sides of her new Quickie surround her like walls. She slumps; her legs drag on the foot pedals and frequently pop off in spasms; her head droops to her chest, tired after the effort of keeping it steady.

I tilt the chair backward, ease the front wheels over the stoop, then pick the back of the chair up and over. I'm a pro. Hasn't most of my life been a preparation for this? Bleakly, I recall my mother's chair and the many times I'd done the same for her.

Home is a small rental on Third Avenue, in an area of Salt Lake known as The Avenues, renowned for historical Victorians and Prairie bungalows. Mine is Victorian, turn-of-the-century, red brick with leaded windows. The honey-colored hardwood floors are covered with my rugs—eclectic kelims, my favorite of which is one I'd just brought back from Mexico, orange and gold with little triangles of lime green. There is a living room, a dining room, and a small study filled with my books, a desk, and a futon for visitors. The bedroom, even smaller, just about holds my queen-sized bed and a TV. Tim is still downstairs in the basement "quarters," but we rarely see Tim these days. He has his responsibilities, he tells me; I wonder meanly what else he's been responsible for.

Rachel, who'd moved her stuff to the house on Third Avenue months before her accident, had once considered living in the basement. At the time, I thought she might be happier in the study near the bathroom. (Oh, the indolence of those former days!) Now I move her into my room, where I plan to share the bed until she gets oriented. And with the memory problem, who knows how long that will take?

I arrange her clothes in my drawers and closet, crammed together with my own stuff. We are both clotheshorses and have more than we ever wear anyway. Rachel, the jock, must own forty T-shirts, and I am one for jeans, jeans in all colors with various designer labels glued on a buttock. I begin to fling things into a heap on the floor and stuff dark green garbage bags for the thrift shops. Rachel lounges on my bed and asks me questions: *What* year is it again? *What* was it again that happened to me? The inflections are a good sign, I figure, an indication that she knows these questions have been asked and answered before. She will not be like Mr. M.

MR. M. IS THE pseudonym for a real-life person who suffered total memory obliteration at the hands of a surgeon
who was trying to cure his epilepsy. Mr. M. appears often in
casebooks about brain injuries, and the chilling story of Mr.
M. has been eloquently documented by Philip J. Hilts in a
book called *Memory's Ghost*. According to Hilts, Mr. M.'s surgeon drilled two small holes into his cranium with a hand-
cranked rotary drill, inserted a silver straw and sucked out
the mid-portion of his brain, called the hippocampus, as well
as all the surrounding matter and formations. As Hilts puts
it, "In one sharp intake of air, [Mr. M.] had lost the world,"
meaning that he lost the ability to recall anything at all—not
faces, not names, not places, not events—though his epilepsy
improved slightly. After a long period of time, he apparently
recognized his mother, but that was it.

No, Rachel would not be as severely impaired as Mr. M.
She remembers people, not only from her past, by name,
always and consistently, but even those she'd met since the
accident, at least by face. Well, no surprise there—I am convinced that Rachel has a special neuron cluster reserved just
for people, a biochemical blessing her mother positively
lacks. Though her college graduation seems to be a "hole" as
is her trip to Italy, she remembers most of her past. This,
mostly without anecdote, sadly; that is to say, she recalls the
shape of her past, a kind of historical narrative, without the
specific episodes that give the past richness.

But, even from the beginning, with cues, Rachel *could*
occasionally remember some present facts. We had rhymes
in those days. We called 1996 "the year of the sticks," so when
I said "year of the sticks," Rachel would say, *"Ninety-six!"*
Although she sometimes couldn't remember Dr. Frank's

name, if I said *Frr*—, she'd supply the missing *—ank* quite
confidently. I'd read somewhere that the hippocampus was
responsible for a certain kind of *aha!* memory, and it seemed
to me that Rachel's hippocampus was at least functioning.
With visual or auditory clues, Rachel was able to pull something out of somewhere, though not consistently.

In Rachel's case, unlike Mr. M.'s, *some* of her experiences
bypassed short-term memory and found their way into long-
term memory, from which she was able to retrieve them. I
say *some* experiences, because not all, not even *most* experiences landed in that long-term vat at this point in time. This
was bizarre. For example, she would be totally blank five
minutes after, say, a trip to the mall, but a day later might
recall it. What synaptical short circuit caused that magical
retrieval? (I envisioned a little troop of wrong-headed neuro-
transmitters creeping slowly around axons, bypassing those
short-term synapses, finding their clever way to some home
base, like lemmings.)

Also, her procedural memory seemed to be intact. She
remembered how to do things, like make a sandwich and zip
up a jacket. And she'd added new procedures post-accident,
like helping with the transfers from her chair and eating left-
handed.

It is events that seemed to bypass her entirely—and by
this I mean literally everything that happened to her: conversation (even seconds later), meals (she never remembered if
she had eaten recently or not, except by feeling around in her
mouth with her tongue), outings, visits. All gone gone gone.
And in this, she was indeed like Mr. M.

"Everything is skewed a little to the left," she used to say
in those early homecoming days. Or: "I feel like I'm in a

dream." This latter feeling has often been reported by amnesiacs—the feeling that their waking life is fuzzy and dreamlike, the world, like Mr. M's, "bursting out of a wall of mist." I took to watching Rachel's eyes when she tried to recall something (unsuccessfully). They seemed to gaze toward the upper left rather than the upper right like mine did; and so I conceived some amateurish theories having to do with her eye movement and memory. I'm still not sure my theories were wrong, but they most certainly were amateurish and, anyway, I had no way to change her eye movement even if I were right.

But the memory deficit, right from the beginning, was our main plague. As the days wore on, Dr. Frank's pronouncement haunted me. And so, I'm chagrined to say, did the social worker's unkind prediction that it would only get worse. It *was* worse for me—I was exhausted, nervous, frightened. I felt as if someone had dropped us both off a cliff (tied together, of course) into a dangerous sea, as if it was only a matter of time before we'd pull each other under.

Though her spastic bladder had improved somewhat—I call it a spastic bladder, a condition that was confirmed a year later, but in those days the doctors thought it had to do with memory—she still felt the urge to pee too many times throughout the night. This was no easy operation. As it was, the room was too small for both of us plus all the apparatus. The space between the bathroom door and the side of the bed was barely large enough to contain the wheelchair, rendering that entry virtually impassable. Half-asleep, I'd grab her under the arms, drag her to a seated position and push her legs down off the bed; then, with her left hand still clinging too tightly to my neck (for months I was dizzy from this tricky maneuver), I pulled her up and swung her into the wheelchair. Then came the difficult job of jockeying the chair around so we could enter the bathroom facing the right way for the toilet. An hour later, we'd repeat this operation. And so on, into the night.

In the mornings we'd both be exhausted. I'd fix breakfast, hardly daring to leave Rachel alone at the table. The one time I did, she slipped from her chair and I found her half-up and half-down, nightgown tangled at her neck. Those days were like a war zone—each minute required an intensity of focus I could barely muster. "Everydayness" seemed unattainable, lucky, and almost a little superficial—as if those who were destined to walk that carefree road had been deprived a profounder experience.

The hardest thing, after the more obviously debilitating nighttimes, was her perseveration. Over and over again, she'd ask what had happened, where she was, how old she was, whether she had graduated from college, what year it was. I'd answer questions while pouring milk into her cereal—*you're in Salt Lake City, you were in a motorcycle accident, you're twenty-five, it's 1996*—and as she took the first spoonful, she'd be asking them all over again. *Where am I? What happened to me?* I felt I was being tortured. Once or twice, I broke down and sobbed, begging her to stop. Finally I typed a list of all her questions and all her answers. "Read your list," I'd say, thrusting it into her left hand. But it took her a long time to read that three-page list, and, by the time she got to the end, she'd forgotten three-quarters of it. *What happened to me?* she'd ask faintly. *Just tell me.*

Guadalupe, help us, I'd pray, prostrating myself before her image—this one a kitsch trompe l'oeil that oscillated between the Virgin and a suffering Christ figure, striped with silver foil.

A TEAM OF THERAPISTS arrived each day to work on her activities of daily living (ADLs), as well as speech (which included cognitive memory work) and physical and occupational therapies. Molly had gotten Rachel to stand up between the parallel bars in the hospital therapy room, and now our new therapist, Sherry, a motherly woman with a bright blond coif, had her standing at the sink doing dishes with her left hand. Rachel was in high spirits with the therapists around— they were all "Girlfriend" to her. She loved an audience. *Shake-shake-shake, shake your bootay,* she was apt to sing while standing up, propped against the sink or table or wall. Or, *Girlfriend, you've got it going on.* After they left, she'd be despondent. "I hate fucking therapy," she'd say.

"You didn't seem to hate it. You seemed to be having a good time."

"Was I?"

"You were, you were. You shook your bootay. You had everyone laughing."

"I did? What did I do?"

"Besides shaking the bootay—?"

"The stanky bootay—"

"Besides shaking the excellent, stanky bootay, you asked for a big-assed cup of coffee."

"I did? What else did I do?"

"I can't remember."

"Oh ha ha ha. Well, I do. Therapy sucks."

But if physical therapy enraged her, speech and cognitive therapy enraged her even more. To be confronted by her mental lapses and incapacities must have been a horror. The speech therapist, Margaret, was a slim, elegantly dressed, compassionate woman who, unfortunately, did not share Rachel's sense of humor. She spoke to Rachel in an amplified tone, enunciating each word as you might when speaking to a foreign, hearing-impaired person. "Good after-noon, Rach-el," she would say. And Rachel would, not so discreetly, roll her eyes. "Shall we play some games? Would you like that, Rach-el?"

"What-ev-er," Rachel would say, with a mockery that bypassed the therapist. When Margaret presented flash cards for identification, Rachel was insulted. Identifying objects was not a problem for Rachel. Asked to identify a picture of a plate of spaghetti, she pretended not to get it. "Ahhhh," she'd say, thinking it over. "Fruit cocktail?" Then: "Only kidding, Girlfriend, I fucking know it's pasta alfredo."

But when they got to the memory games, Rachel was at sea. She fumed, not remembering what she vowed she could. And she resisted writing things down. "My right hand's on strike and my left hand sucks at penmanship" was her excuse.

"We're trying to find the *way* in which Rachel remembers," the therapist told me, explaining that everyone has different ways of remembering—visual, aural, tactile, and so on. Rachel, she speculated, stored things creatively, complexly, and this was why her memory was so slow to recover. I tried to reason it out: How *would* Rachel, *my* daughter, remember? Me, I'm associative rather than logical. In conversation, I find myself flitting from topic to topic, disposed, organically it seems, to digression. I imagine my mind, and because of genetics, perhaps, Rachel's, zigzagging blithely across neurons, from *a* to *n* to *f*. We are not orderly types. Even now, Rachel will be waylaid by a pun, thrown off the logical, narrative track by any old incongruity. But, unlike me, she can't find her way back again.

MEMORY, ACCORDING TO HENRI Bergson, occupies the space between mind and body. It conveys mind to body and body to mind. It gives us our quality of life—makes possible, in other words, the narratives that keep our lives going forward to the next thing. If the thing is not *next* it loses its richness—isolated and unlinked to a history, it becomes meaningless, even ridiculous. Biologically and neurologically, we are creatures of context, of narrative.

Consider the activity of the neurons or brain cells. Unlike the body's cells, which divide and multiply, microcosmically illustrating the propagation of the species, neurons are systems of communication. Their most salient features are a clutch of dendrites that branch out to receive information across the synapses between cells, and a single long axon that reaches to the synapse—literally the space between neurons—through which chemical and electrical information is conveyed to the next cell.

By nature, then, the activity of the neuron is narrative, metonymic, associative. The information conveyed by each neuron accumulates along a complex circuitry of neurons and produces a thought, a corresponding action in the mind. If the information that passes from neuron to neuron is somehow tampered with—if the transmitters or receptors

are artificially altered by drugs or disease, for example—
memory at its very biological foundation will be altered or
even incapacitated. We are hardwired into narrative; it is, I
would go so far to say, the ground and not merely the consequence of memory.

And so I began to see striking correspondences between
brain theory and the theories of narrative I taught at least
once a year to my grad students. This complex subject, which
analyzes, among other things, narrative structure, narrative
style, and narrative digression, could easily be a study of the
brain itself. An individual author's style and chosen structure
might be a kind of map of the brain, I conjectured, pointing
to the unique operation of a particular brain and, therefore, to
the way a person remembers. Or, conversely, a style or structure might put into operation particular brain activities—a
progress or regress along this or that line of synapses, a burst
of seratonin here, a little less dopamine there. Who knew? I
was a neophyte in the brain game. My speculations ranged
wildly (a map, perhaps, of my own brain's ebbs and flows).

It occurred to me, too, that without the compulsive activities of confabulation and perseveration, a written narrative
(much less a fiction) of any interest could not be made at all.
This memoir I am trying to write, a loose weave of my half-
lit half-memories, which become clearer as I write them
down, is an effect of confabulation. Any good narratologist
will tell you that when we articulate our lives, we are already
in the arena of fiction—the self of the past being essentially
unrecoverable. Thus, what we call "memory" must be an
imaginative act, configured always on the gap of forgetfulness, assembled from bits and pieces of who-knows-what.

Likewise, I perseverate. I return obsessively to certain

themes, to certain rhetorical strategies. Style is always the effect of perseveration, the best of which is a kind of inspired repetition that allows the reader a glimpse into the speaker's mind. In fiction, it is invaluable for creating character (in nonfiction, voice). Consider this perseverative bit from Donald Barthelme's "The Falling Dog": "A dog jumped on me out of a high window. I think it was the third floor, or the fourth floor. Or the third floor." In one perseverative loop, we are given the obsessive, possibly brain injured (on account of the falling dog) character.

As I puzzled over these matters, I hit upon the idea that I could do for Rachel what her therapists could not do, perhaps, as *feelingly.* I could become her writing teacher. If I could encourage her to write stories, I reasoned, then perhaps narrative making would jump-start her memory. "Tell me a story, Rachel," I urged. "Make something up." At first, Rachel's stories were nonnarrative confabulations: *There is Justine with a bee on her head.*

"What about Justine? What about the bee?" I prompted.

Rachel smiled, shrugged. "That's it. The end."

Eventually, the stories would acquire a narrative feel, but the narratives would be flat and curiously truncated. *Once upon a time,* she might begin, but then the character Justine or a small, pale, weak girl or whoever would simply drift into some arena—the desert, the city, the mall—and stay there. These stories were shapeless, lacking destinies. Still, a sense of conflict was beginning: built into the notion of "small, pale, weak" is the trajectory of a plot, a sense that the frail will undertake a journey to overcome her frailty (also, perhaps more obviously, a metaphor for Rachel's sense of her injured self).

After a while, her stories attempted some kind of resolution: *A very small weak girl struck out for the desert because she had been left alone and her father and mother had died and there was nothing she could think of to do but go to the desert and weep under a mesquite. On the way there, however, she met a nice friend who happened to be called Charles. He had a bunch of chocolates with him, which he shared with the small weak girl and which revitalized her. They had a great time and eventually they went to Las Vegas. The end.*

"Not bad," I say.

"Really?" says Rachel, pleased.

"It shows you're optimistic, too—I mean, that you think chocolates could cure the small, weak girl."

"What was the story again?"

MEANWHILE, IN AN IRONY only real life can provide, *I* can't stop remembering. On the refrigerator are pictures of Rachel before her accident. To take them down seems a violation, as if I were erasing the old Rachel from my life. To leave them up is an excruciating reminder.

There she is wearing a black afro wig, red high heels, and shorts, aping for the camera. What I love about this picture is the obvious grace of that runner's body, hips twisted, one knee bent, her good calf muscles shining. And here she is in Paris, just last year, sitting on a wall, backpack next to her in a heap, legs dangling, while behind her dazzles the beautiful city. Or this one, framed by flowers in Ecuador, a basket in her arms. She is uncannily photogenic, and, when I look into her face, I realize this is what I miss the most: this direct, unself-conscious gaze, full of intelligence and candor.

Though now her face itself is miraculously intact—no facial paralysis; well, maybe a little tug on the left side when she's laughing really, really hard—whatever animated it has gone under. Like a Christmas tree with the lights out, she is glowless.

A photo of the two of us taken last summer brings back a rush of memories. On our famous road trip to Tucson, we'd stopped at a gas station and asked a stranger to snap us in our matching Gap overalls. We'd bought the overalls days before, on what Rachel wryly referred to as one of our "mother-daughter bonding experiences": a trip to the mall. Later, in some shop, a salesclerk referred to Rachel as my "friend," and I, flattered, had not corrected her. Rachel was miffed. "Why did you do that?" she wanted to know. Sorry, Rache.

In my favorite photo, she has her arm around me in San Miguel, smiling confidently at the camera, posed against the blue tiles of the first *casita* we rented in Mexico; and I am smiling too. What if, by some strange magic, I had known the future then? Would I have been smiling? But I can't bear this game I play with myself, matching my memory of that time with the reality of this one. Why do I do it? Why do I prod these memories, like worrying a sore tooth? In the next room, she is doing range-of-motion exercises with her occupational therapist, for god's sake, and here I am weeping.

9

*We are sealed vessels afloat upon what it is convenient to call
reality; at some moments, without a reason, without an effort,
the sealing matter cracks; in floods reality . . .*
                           —Virginia Woolf, *Moments of Being*

WHATEVER ELSE IS DAMAGED in Rachel since her accident,
"the shopping gene," as we call it in our family, has been
mercifully spared. Rachel loves to go to the mall. Unlike
most brain injured, Rachel doesn't sleep much during the
day, and so the mall, in those early days, is a blessing. I push
her on the varnished bricks of Trolley Square, and, because
she's on their level, she greets every little kid she sees. *Hey
cutie pie, hey silly-billy*, she's apt to say, reaching out for any
small head that passes within fondling distance. The
response is various. Most kids smile happily, intuiting, as
only kids can do, a simpatico spirit. But some shrink away,

fearful or repulsed, and this pains me. I find myself catching their mothers' eyes in brief apology; I tell Rachel to hush.

My reaction is complicated and makes me feel vaguely wrong. When I scrutinize it, I realize that I can't stand seeing it dawn on people that there's something *off* about Rachel. Brain injury is supposed to be an invisible ailment, since most brain injured are physically unimpaired. But in addition to her physical handicap, Rachel's disinhibition makes only too clear that her sense of propriety has vanished, that there is some pathology compelling her friendliness. If not normal, I want her to at least *appear* normal—in this way, I can pretend she *is* normal.

"Stop talking to everyone," I hiss, squeezing her shoulder. Years later, I will still be begging her to restrain herself. Once, not long ago I explained that when she was over-friendly, she signaled to people that there was something wrong with her. She thought about it a minute, then said, shaming me, "Well, there *is* something wrong with me."

And here in the mall she's in seventh heaven. When I stop to finger the material of a jacket in Banana Republic, she scuttles away, one-footed, propelling herself over to racks of drawstring pants and baseball caps. In a while, her lap will be laden with three hundred dollars' worth of scarves, purses, T-shirts, shorts, and a silver bracelet. "Forget about it," I say, thrusting the tangled clump back into the arms of the puzzled sales clerk. "Sorry, Girlfriend," she tells the salesclerk. "Sorry about that." The salesclerk doesn't mind; she's one of the smitten, already enamored of Rachel. "She's so adorable," she whispers to me. And how do I feel about that? Okay, I guess. I buy her the bracelet and a baseball hat.

———

"YOU ARE MY MEMORY," Rachel tells me, and it's true. I remember the actual as well as I can, and what I don't remember I shamelessly invent. "You got up, you brushed your teeth, your therapists came over and you stood up; you went to the mall, you bought a hat, you ate frozen yogurt—vanilla, chocolate, and coffee with Oreo cookie crumbs."

"What will we do tomorrow?" she worries. She has less tolerance for the uncertainty of the future than the rest of us. "What do I have to do?" she says. We make lists of questions and answers; we record her voice and her day's activities as they occur into a palm-sized device called a voice organizer; we plan; we talk. Together we assemble an imperfect representation, a narrative we can rely on nonetheless, one which compels us forward to the next thing.

On Sunday we attend mass at the Newman Center. An unforgettable experience (though, of course, Rachel forgets it): A lapsed Catholic, I haven't been to mass in years, but Rachel wants to go, and what with my indebtedness to Guadalupe, who am I to refuse? The Newman Center is a cosy, if uninspired, community building, replete with cinder-block walls and goodwill. The best part is the politics, liberal, pro-choice, pro–sexual preference, my kind of church. We sit on bridge chairs and watch a small guitar trio sing and play a few dreary folk songs. Suddenly Rachel starts to giggle. "Look," she says *sotto voce,* pointing to the folk trio. "My doctor is moonlighting as a guitar player." And sure enough, there is Dr. Frank, strumming away, in the same no-nonsense manner with which she dispenses medical pronouncements. But I am elated! It's been two weeks since our hospital departure and RACHEL RECOGNIZES DR. FRANK!

Later in the mass, she distinguishes herself again: In this church, the congregation is invited to speak their own intentions during the prayer, a ritual I don't remember from the old days, but which at this moment holds great appeal for Rachel. Head craning conspicuously to see each speaker, mouth working in a bemused, silent rehearsal, she is revving up for her own spoken intention. *"Don't say anything,"* I whisper, but Rachel is undeterred. Her voice, I should mention, no longer that tiny whisper of weeks ago, has found itself—a bit flat and uninflected, and higher than before, but clear as a bell.

"FOR ALL THE BRAIN DAMAGED, WHEREVER THEY MAY BE," she says, briefly stunning the entire congregation for a beat or two before they join in with the response, *Lord hear our prayer.* I don't know whether to laugh or cry.

I AM THINKING about Mr. M.'s mother. It was she who authorized the surgery which would take his memory from him. They are said to have fought bitterly. Once she hit him; another time, he threw a fork at her. After a long separation, however, they were said to have embraced "movingly." When she died, it was Mr. M. who found her on the kitchen floor, and he simply sat by her until, by chance, someone arrived.

Without any memory at all, Mr. M. was treated by hospital workers as a sort of benign pet. As Hilts puts it, chillingly, without memory, Mr. M. had lost his "humanity." I do not want Rachel to lose her humanity. I do not want her to be treated like a pet. Mr. M.'s story terrifies me. I do not want Rachel to find me on the kitchen floor.

Motherhood in our culture carries with it a burden of guilt, and it is this burden of guilt that is made unbearable by a sick child. It is the mother's job to keep a child of any age healthy and safe; only then can she retire to her bedroom and read a book. Months after the accident, I catch myself investigating my conscience for a way to take the blame for all of it. True, I had forbidden motorcycles and insisted on bicycle helmets, but what if I had allowed Rachel to come to San Miguel after Italy? She wanted to. She asked. But I said, no, she'd had her trip, and wasn't I coming home a few weeks after her return? It didn't make sense, I said. And so she went to Steamboat Springs instead. I know, even now, that I was reasonable; but it is a lingering and painful knowledge that with the right kind of unreasonableness, I might have saved her.

I met a woman recently who has a child with Down's syndrome. A young woman whom I had known slightly before the birth of her son, she seemed to have aged twenty years. She looked drained after years of caring for, working with, fighting on behalf of her child. She wanted, she told me, the very best for him, adding that she never thought she was doing her best. What is this weight placed on the shoulders of mothers that requires from them all that they have? I was giving Rachel all (or most) that I had, but I knew it was insufficient, would always be insufficient. If I could trade places with her, I would. If I thought that hurling myself off a cliff would help her, I'd do it. But hurling myself off a cliff or giving up boyfriends—in Denver, I'd actually pledged this—or quitting my job wouldn't allow Rachel to run up City Creek Canyon again or bring her memory back. And,

like the mother of Mr. M., I have my moments. "SHUT
UP!" I scream at Rachel after a particularly excruciating perseverative bout. "YOU'VE SAID THE SAME THING
TWENTY TIMES!" And then I think, what awful pass
have we come to that I now scream at the person I love so
dearly? I had not been a screamer; I was the laid-back,
relaxed mom, permissive, understanding, unshockable. And
who am I now?

And so you must imagine the bewildered mother pacing
the floor as Rachel knuckles under for therapy, tearing her
fingernails until they bleed, smoking. The mother trailed by
a dim sense of guilt. The mother whose family now thinks
she is a marvel. The mother who quips, "From black sheep
to saint in thirty seconds of catastrophe." The mother who
lacks the required stamina for this job.

AND WHAT OF TIM, the phantom in the basement? He
drifted in and out of the house, sitting with Rachel from time
to time, usually at breakfast before going to work, not to
return until the wee hours. His relationship with Rachel was
what you'd expect: confused. He was affectionate toward
her, holding her hand, kissing her avuncularly on the forehead. That part was all right. But his expectations were even
more inflated than mine.

One night he took her on a date. Her friend Karen Sahn
was visiting from Denver and she went along too. When
they returned from dinner, Rachel and Tim looked shaken,
upset. Karen reported that he had been "on her case"
throughout the meal, badgering her about her table manners, admittedly appalling, and about her inappropriate

comments to the waiter. I couldn't blame him, on one hand. On the other, I wanted to murder him.

Then there was the Saturday in late February when I left him in charge for a few hours while I went off to see a friend's play at Salt Lake Community Theater. Halfway through the first act, I was filled with foreboding. I left the theater, propelled by intuition. When I walked in the door, there was Tim screaming at Rachel to try harder. There was Rachel sobbing. "That's it," I said, "you're history." And that is when Tim walked out of our lives forever.

A month or so later, after Tim had already left the Salt Lake vicinity, I hired a lawyer to see if we could recover anything from the accident. A month or so after that, I received a cordial letter from the firm informing me that we had no worthwhile case to pursue, and saying that both the police and the witness, whom they had contacted, had confirmed Tim's culpability. He was driving recklessly and too fast; there were no telephone company cones in the road, no impediments of any kind.

Now Tim, recall, had told us this very cogent story at Denver General when my daughter was in a coma, when he was sleeping on the waiting room floor swaddled in a blanket for his sins. This story—this lie—had endeared him to us. "Fuck you, Tim C———," Rachel will still say, years after her injury. And Tim, if he ever reads this book, should know that.

THE WINTER QUARTER with my graduate creative writing class would go on until March. I taught the class on Monday nights under the fluorescent lights of a seminar room in the Languages and Communications building. For Rachel I hired Mike, the partner of Connie, one of my grad students. An ex-pro hockey player, soon-to-be attorney with a dry wit, Mike, I imagined, would be perfect for Rachel. Mike also helped out during the day, from time to time, when I needed to sleep after a bad night shift. But Rachel disliked being, as she put it, "pawned off on a babysitter." And Mike, I had to admit, was a little low-key for Rachel in those days. She complained that he wasn't funny enough, didn't talk enough. Today, she finds Mike hilarious, which is indicative of her recovery, but in those days, Connie was more her style. Like me, Connie was able to follow her into absurdity, match her puns and better them—and they had the same taste in shoes. When Connie and Rachel went shopping, I could be assured Rache would come home with orange shoes or purple shoes or shoes with big square toes or polka-dotted, buckled, ruffled, sparkled shoes, happy as a lark.

Because she was so miserable when I taught my once-a-week grad class—Monday evenings, from six to ten—I decided to teach the class at home. I moved all fifteen of us into my living room—dragging chairs and pillows from every nook and cranny—where we would settle in for a four-hour session. And although Rachel would eventually sleep, she'd always appear several times, like the madwoman in *Jane Eyre*, offering a wiseass suggestion or simply interrupting with some joke. Once she scuttled out in her chair, the sides of her nightgown flapping open like two wings, exposing her naked self. "NO!" I shouted, panic seizing my heart as I scooted her back into the bedroom and tucked her in.

While others laughed gently, humoring Rachel in her outlandishness, I found myself tightening inside, which made me feel old. *Hush* and *Stop* were sometimes the only words I spoke when we were in any kind of group. But, of course, Rachel wouldn't hush or stop because she mostly had a kindly, if somewhat coerced, audience.

Alone, I was at my best with Rachel, snuggling at least two-thirds of the time, our bodies cradled into each other, her head on my chest, holding hands, smooching, laughing. "These snuggles are very important for my recovery," Rachel still says, only a little tongue-in-cheek. I suppose if recovery is linked to bliss, this might be true—from the corner of my eye I'd catch her little half-smile of ecstasy, as if she were in the throes of a heavenly massage or a chocolate sundae. Strangely, with my arms around Rachel I was capable of deep sleep, almost as if drugged.

Other times, I resurrected my stand-up-comic self, inventing funny voices and characters for Rachel's amusement, a meager little talent I'd abandoned in adolescence. The dim-witted caregiver who misunderstood any request, the strict Germanic nurse who insisted on absurd protocols of hygiene, the guy who gave "high fo's" instead of "high fives," the hapless woman who could never complete her sentences. "Do you want some ———?" "How about if we go ———?" (This last I stole from Rachel's journal, pre-injury, when she reported having spent an evening at an Aspen club confounding people with sentence fragments.)

But if I won the goofy character award, Rachel was at her best with sheer verbal wit. When, to be funny, I deliberately put the Kleenex box she'd asked for just out of reach, she came up with a hilarious title for my next book, *How to Abuse the Handicapped*. And, in a turn that showed her insight as well as her finely tuned sense of the incongruous, she created a category called "brain-damaged humor"—

pointless riddles or jokes that were always just a hair off. *What has two wings and flies? A sandwich.* I especially liked her subcategory "brain-damaged clichés"—*cross my heart and hope to attack*; *in one fell spoke.* Her wit soared way beyond my own, her synapses working rapid-fire when it came to anything linguistic (though who would find these amusing besides us two, I had no idea).

In those days, a real conversation was virtually impossible, so I relied on games like this to keep us both going. Also, we played more serious (i.e., more therapeutic) games, like trying to name a wacky item for each letter of the alphabet; and though she had to be reoriented continually during this game, what she came up with—*blubber, dishrag, ectoplasm*—was always a delight. I wondered if her impressive language skills had to do with disinhibition—if without that frontal lobe brake, she was free to speak her mind in a way that the average twenty-five-year-old was not.

Her perceptions about people seemed an elaboration of this ability: "So-and-so probably has a wardrobe totally composed of beige." But here was the mystery: How did she remember so accurately and wittily the essence of each person?

IF MEMORY IS BOOSTED by the gap of forgetfulness, then what we don't recall is as crucial to the narrative of remembering as what we do. When I think back to our road trip to Tucson, for example, it's amazing how much I've forgotten. I remember driving in the car with Rachel at the wheel; I remember the photograph at the gas station (or was it a restaurant?), but have no memory of who, exactly, snapped that photo, male or female, young or old. I could probably, in writing, recapture the spirit of that beautiful drive south, from the dark green pines of northern Utah to the red and green canyons in the south, the rolling hills that gave way to scrub oak that gave way to the flat, desert plains of Arizona with those low, charcoal-colored mountains undulating like water against the sky. It is a fact that I remember almost nothing of what we did once we got to Tucson. Surviving in my mind is only a single image: Right before we began the long trek back to Salt Lake, Rachel holding Maddy, one-armed on her right hip in front of my red Nissan; and what I remember most is Maddy's face, her cherubic blondness, like a little halo roosting on her head, and her round, blue eyes. Though as I prod my memory—this writing is a memory prod—suddenly comes a clear recollection of sharing the guest house bedroom with Rachel, her clothes strewn annoyingly on the floor, the kids jumping on us too early in the morning, and Rachel and Nick playing a game with pillows.

The mystery is this: How do I manage to create what we call memory from such scant traces? And why can't Rachel? Is it the traces that are missing or some profounder apparatus?

Virginia Woolf's metaphor for the experience of individual consciousness is a sealed vessel bobbing on a huge sea which she calls reality. Every once in a while, for Woolf, the "sealing matter" breaks and a little reality seeps in. Woolf's metaphor, it turns out, is not so far removed from the theories of cognitive psychologists which contend that we experience and thus remember only a fraction of the world around us—that we are fundamentally enclosed consciousnesses needing only a trickle of reality to fuel our subjectivities. If this is so, I could imagine two leaks in Rachel's sealed ves-

ed to me), not only could Rachel not remember those
things, she could not recall having been asked to memo-
them. Well, I could have predicted that.

Meanwhile, Rachel is becoming more and more dis-
ed. She knows this is a terrible, humiliating experience,
visit with Dr. Frank, and she will know it for hours,
—not the details, of course, not even the event itself,
gh it will sit with her like a bad taste in the mouth, this
essing afternoon.

he next day, I call Dr. Deb Wagner, a woman whose
usiasm and compassion for her patients has caught my
tion in the past few months. A colleague and friend of
Frank, she nonetheless agrees to take Rachel on. She
s Rachel is great, she tells me. She'd love to work with
She would even speak to Dr. Frank. That was easy! I
, wondering why I hadn't contacted Dr. Wagner earlier
ctually looking forward to our appointment.

NTH AND A HALF post-homecoming: Rachel has moved
er own sleeping quarters in the study. Her bladder
ms come and go, but nighttimes are much more tran-
She has graduated from home therapy to an outpatient
a few miles away. There she works with therapists for
I hours and meets with other brain injured, in various
of recovery.

e hates interacting with the brain injured. She simply
ee herself as one of them—or, possibly, she sees herself
arly as one them and this is unbearable to her.
casionally, an aide provides transport to the facility,

sel—one that let reality in and one that quickly, almost
instantaneously, let most of it stream out again. Except for
those times when something "sticks," as it were: a wayward
trickle of a trickle holing up in the odd neuronal estuary.

But my interpretation of Woolf's model is too simplistic.
For in Rachel, what's missing seems to be a chunk of subjec-
tivity crucial to narrative making. As if forgetfulness were no
longer the rich experience it is for most of us. As if the sealed
vessel itself had met with disaster.

WHEN THE UNIVERSITY of Arizona invites me to give a
keynote speech for a critical theory conference, I am resistant
at first. Critical theory is, at this point, the farthest thing from
my mind. But they are inviting me both as a theorist and as a
fiction writer, which gives me some leeway. Also, they are
offering me a generous honorarium, too generous, in fact, to
turn down. It occurs to me I might write something on brain
theory and narrative theory, since this is what's been on my
mind. And I might factor in some of Rachel's story.

So I write a talk called, most academically (to give it
credibility), "Dream, Memory, Story and the Recovery of
Narrative." I write it in Tim's old basement room, which I've
converted into an office. Upstairs, the therapists are urging
Rachel to her feet, and here I am downstairs, writing about
it. It's an odd experience, writing about a life event as the life
event unfolds above my head:

*Still my head buzzes unpleasantly. There are worries. There
are undecided questions and shaky transitions and thoughts right
now that I have trouble completing. I'd like you to know that I'm
writing this in my basement under these bare bulbs that hurt my*

*eyes and that it's snowing outside and that I can hear the creak of
Rachel's wheelchair overhead—she's put on rap again—and that
I just quit smoking. I want to say this is not a memoir (too messy)
and not a theory (too untheoretical) and not a fiction (too true)
and that it occurs to me that the buzzing in my head is due to
radon, probably, and that it's cold in the basement and I detest
snow and that like Rachel I ask, why why why? Why me?*

*Because it's unbelievable, isn't it, when life suddenly assumes
the grotesque and overblown proportions of dreams? But which
is the construction, the dream or the life? It occurs to me that we
approach our dreams like "fiction," like impossibilities, that
we've divided dream from life in order to preserve the smooth,
untroubled narrative of our dailiness. Rachel, for example, frequently feels that she's in a dream or is waking from a dream. She
asks: Is this reality? And I think that her reality is literally unbelievable to her—she cannot conceive of it.*

ONE MONTH POST-HOMECOMING, Rachel has her first outpatient appointment with Dr. Frank. In her office, the doctor
has a bowl of wrapped candy bars of every denomination,
which Rachel immediately plunders, tearing off the wrap-
pings one-handed and stuffing huge, unwholesome chunks
into her mouth faster than you can say *Milky Way*. Dr. Frank
sits sternly behind her desk, Rachel's file open in front of her.

"Okay, Rachel," she begins. "I'm going to give you three
things to remember: *Orange, Chicken, Airplane*. In a little
while, I'll ask you to remember them. Got that?"

"No problem," says Rachel, who like most amnesiacs has
zero insight into her memory difficulties.

I do most of the talking, describing Rachel's progress dur-

ing our first month. And if I err a bit
reporting more positive than negative ev
testing that Rachel has not regressed on
real voice has now displaced that madd
standing and even taking a few steps with
eight-hundred-dollar item is, to my mi
replete with a little rubber seat for rest
deep basket); and, remarkably, since
dependent, she is oriented to our home ar
of all, she seems, I point out to Dr. Fr
"with-it." This ineffable with-it-ness is
photograph submerged in developer be
in stages, so Rachel's submerged glow is g

Dr. Frank listens to my spiel deadpa
few notes in the file, the content of whic
mother continues to have unrealistic inter
rehabilitation; *mother, with her advance*
can outguess the doctors; or simply *mot*
liability.

Without comment, she turns to Rac
dent of the United States, Rachel?"

Rachel's answer is a query: "Clinton

"And before that?"

"Bush?"

"And before that?"

"Reagan?"

"And before that?

"Uh, I don't know, Girlfriend—Nix

It was almost as if the doctor was tryin
scribbling of notes in file, then, "Can you
things I asked you to remember?" To h

and Rachel shares a ride with a young man who is so severely aphasic that he is incapable of uttering a single intelligible word. It pains me to say that his very presence in the world fills Rachel with horror, which translates to contempt. Despite the fact that this young man—who fell off a roof— retains his excellent math and computer skills, has no short-term memory problems and no physical handicap, Rachel sees him as being far more impaired than she is and complains bitterly about being "grouped" with this "moron." Oh, we are partners in denial, my daughter and I, but every once in a while a little reality trickles in.

There is the evening Elena calls, irate about Rachel's behavior. She'd been intolerably rude and insensitive to the boy who'd fallen off the roof. "We can't have this behavior," Elena informed me angrily. All I could do was sputter an apology—this was not the old Rachel, I assured her. Rachel had been compassionate and sensitive to a fault. This was the brain injury, psychological denial, neurological disinhibition. NOT A PARENTING PROBLEM, I wanted to add. WHAT THE HELL WAS I SUPPOSED TO DO ABOUT IT? But I, with frontal lobe intact, did not say this.

THE DAUGHTER IS asking questions. The daughter is saying she wants to die. The mother is wearing out. She is sick of going to the mall. She has wrenched her arm lifting the wheelchair in and out of the car trunk. Likewise her hip. She cannot concentrate, loses important items, forgets appointments, forgets what she was going to say. Now the mother's prayers are for herself: *Give me stamina. Help me do a good job. Help me be a good mother.* Guadalupe stares back at her from her perch on the kitchen wall, from her perch on the TV table, from her perch next to the bathroom mirror.

DR. WAGNER IS astounded by Rachel's progress. She says, "I don't know what you guys are doing, but keep doing it." We are thrilled with her, too. Lanky, athletic, clear-eyed, Deb could be the sporty model on a ski poster, and she seems instantly to know what Rachel needs. "Get her in the gym," she tells me. "Get her up on the stationary bike, the tread-mill, whatever." She tests Rachel's spasticity and decides to give her botox injections right then and there. These injec-tions of minute quantities of a protein toxin produced by the botulism bacteria kill the nerve cells that keep the muscles rigid, and, for Rachel, they work wonders. She sends her to a physical therapist, an expert in orthotics who will not only fit her for a brace but will eventually cast her right leg. (The Achilles tendon, from months in bed, had indeed shrunk, making walking almost impossible.)

"She needs to walk, she needs to exercise, she needs to get back into her body," Deb advises. Rachel is breathless with happiness after seeing Dr. Wagner. She'd met a kindred spirit. "Rachel," Deb says, during our first meeting, "I'd go crazy too if I were you. I don't blame you for being pissed off." She is proactive; she hasn't given up on Rachel's recov-ery. Best of all, she is thorough. She orders a series of neuro-psych tests, just to see, she says, what we're really dealing with here.

———

THE NEUROPSYCHOLOGIST'S OFFICE is like that of a corporate executive. A small man wearing an impeccable shirt and tie, he sits behind an enormous glass-topped desk. Behind him, on a long table in front of a window that overlooks the valley, are photographs of his family. I count three kids, one wife. I find myself imagining them at home, clustered around the dinner table, bright with conversation, an image that fills me with ambivalence.

Meanwhile, he is speaking to me about Rachel, and I am summarizing her, as if by rote at this point, ticking off her strengths and deficits. "Poor thing," he keeps saying, clucking his tongue sympathetically. *Poor thing?* What kind of response is this? And I haven't heard anyone cluck their tongue since grade school. Nevertheless, we make an appointment for her testing.

On test day, I drop her off. The testing, which will take many hours, will be administered by a grad student. The grad student will give her many cokes during the day, the effect of which makes Rachel antsy and irritable. When I pick her up, she is a mess of nerves, almost hysterical from the testing and, I'm guessing, the cokes. "FUCK THIS WHOLE THING, I JUST WANT TO DIE, I CAN'T STAND MY LIFE, FUCK THAT WOMAN I HATED HER, PLEASE DON'T MAKE ME DO THAT AGAIN, I HATE MY LIFE, I JUST WANT TO DIE, FUCK THIS WHOLE THING, FUCK MY BRAIN INJURY, FUCK YOU TIM C——."

On the way home I get a ticket for speeding in a school zone.

————

IN MAY, RACHEL and I fly to Tucson for the occasion of my keynote speech. At the airport, we are met by Mary Pat who weeps when she sees Rachel in her wheelchair, me pushing her up the long ramp. I'm surprised and delighted at the enthusiastic reception of my talk, which indeed became the "seed" of this book. And it is a dream to be back in Tucson, where Rachel is fully and joyously oriented. But Rachel on a plane in those days is a nightmare of perseveration and restlessness. "Where are we going again, Girlfriend? What's the date? Why are we going there? Tucson? Salt Lake?" After an hour or so of unabated questions, I couldn't be sure if we were coming or going either. And then there was the spastic bladder problem. "You just went!" "I still have to!" "You just went!" "I still have to!"

TOWARD THE END of the quarter I am driving home from the University. Snow covers the campus golf course and the telephone wires and the tops of cars. Even the street is full of dirty slush mixed with icy patches (my car swerves), and the sky is white and heavy, as if it will snow again soon. How absurd, I am thinking, that Rachel and I have to deal with snow, with the treachery of hills in this mountain city, with my job at the University, with any of it at this critical time. How much better if we were in Tucson, where Rachel knows everyone, where there is no snow, no hills.

Just thinking about Tucson cheers me up and I begin to imagine a way we could go there, if only for a year. Why couldn't I take a leave of absence? The simple answer is that I can't afford it. Still, when I get home to relieve Mike, I talk it over with Rachel.

"Tucson! Right on, Girlfriend, when do we go?"

But of course we can't really go, so what am I doing getting us both stirred up? But I'm in a good mood anyway, just imagining it, the relief of a sunny, flat, familiar place: something to wish for, at least.

This is when our Guadalupe chooses to make a dramatic entrance. Almost as if she had swooped down in her star-festooned cape, mid-wish, the phone rings. It's someone from the National Endowment of the Arts informing me that I'd won a fiction fellowship.

This is really the way it happened, just at that moment of wishing. And that is how, in the midst of this extraordinary time, we wound up in Tucson for a year.

10

. . . and once I
was here with my memory

I do know that.
There was a beautiful green bottle full of water

and a square yellow tower.
Later I lost track of things a little . . .
                              —TOM STILLINGER, *"Saluti da Firenze"*

IN AUGUST OF 1979, we moved from the suburbs of New York—lawns, shade trees, white kids—to Tucson, Arizona. Rachel was seven. For Rachel—for all of us—Tucson would be a lucky place. It was here that she began and finished her impressive running career, here that she would study and become fluent in Spanish, here that she would amass not only more than fifty athletic trophies but countless accolades for citizenship, leadership, and sociability. And countless friends. With three powerful older siblings, her challenge was to distinguish herself and this she did. She was, as I wrote in one fictionalized account of her, "our star."

This I felt most acutely, lacking athletic star-quality

myself. When she began to bring home blue ribbons from grade school races, I hadn't paid much attention. It wasn't in the genes. But when, at age eleven, she placed third in the Susan B. Anthony Fun Run at Pima College, competing not only against all ages but also against a few runners from the University of Arizona's nationally renowned team, I began to pay attention.

She ran with an intensity that was hard to forget. Relatively short-legged, she didn't have what coaches refer to as a runner's body. But she had great focus, great will. She ran, as one newspaper article put it, with her heart. She went on to become state champion in high school and an NCAA competitor at the University of Arizona. It is this determination that I count on these days, post-injury: Rachel's ability to beat the odds by sheer stamina—a distance runner's gift.

Now we're back in Rachel's lucky place. From the point of view of her brain injury, Tucson is a logical place to be. With her good long-term memory, Rachel will have no trouble orienting herself—she knows Tucson better than I, after all, having run along every sun-broiled street and canyon at one time or another. And orientation is an important factor in brain injury recovery—the lack of which can produce high anxiety, as it did in Rachel's case, and also, I reason somewhat unscientifically, takes up brainpower better used elsewhere.

Moreover, Tucson is where her father and her stepfather live, where her Aunt Mary Pat, Uncle Peter, and at least one cousin live, where the friends who cheered for her in the past are still cheering her on with their letters, cards, and wishes for a good recovery. *Tucson Daily Star* sports columnist Greg Hanson had given her a headline after the accident. (Rachel:

"Isn't it ironic that it takes a severe brain injury to merit a headline on the sports page?") Nevertheless, TUCSON RUN- NER BATTLES COMA, as well as frequent updates by Greg Hanson, kept the Tucson readership faithfully informed about Rachel's progress. What could be better than Tucson for Rachel? Here she has a whole cheering section and not just one lone mom.

Thanks to the financial generosity of my parents and the willingness of the low-residency Warren Wilson MFA Creative Writing Program to hire me for two semesters—I'd taken a year's leave-of-absence without pay, and even an NEA wouldn't support us for an entire year—we moved into a house on Second Avenue, around the corner from Margot and Steve's postseason home. The streets are flat; there is no snow. Now that her right leg is casted, Rachel is beginning to walk with the aid of her fancy walker. Within a month or so, she'll be cruising up the street to the bagel place, on her own steam.

I am greatly relieved to be here amid the saguaros and ocotillo, though it wasn't so long ago that this landscape struck me as impossibly strange. "It is the only place," a friend once observed, "where the vegetation is more unfriendly than the people." To me, now, the vegetation is enormously comforting. In the way that the familiar always brings with it the illusion of time recovered, the little two-noted *croo-croo* of the mourning doves at six A.M., the dusty smell of the air, and the chunky desert cacti with their shock-ing eruption of bloom almost allow me to fool myself into thinking that the events of the past eight months haven't happened. Or, at least, that they will *stop* happening, that we will arrive at some serendipitous transformation from nightmare to paradise. Hadn't I used a large portion of money from my NEA to ship our household down here? Wasn't this a measure of my faith, indeed *trust*, in the powers of Tucson?

And so our new house, filled with my old possessions, looks just like home. Only bigger. There are three nice-sized bedrooms and two baths; there's a Saltillo-tiled family room and a small back porch overlooking a tidy garden. Here Rachel will have her own bedroom and sleep in her old iron bed, which I retrieve, with John's help, from storage one afternoon. And, as if a final omen of our rosy future, Rachel's best friend, Bridget, needs a place to live and we have just the room for her. We can barbeque. We can have parties. We can recover in every sense of the word—what's lost, what's past, what's injured.

RIGHT AWAY RACHEL is more oriented in Tucson. In the car, she gives me directions, which is a thrill.

"Take Tucson Boulevard, Girlfriend, it's much shorter." She wears her baseball cap backward, her trademark headgear, cranks up the AC and KRQ on the radio and sings along with the popular songs I'll never know how she learns.

"Turn right at the stop sign, Casserole-head," she instructs. "Slow down now."

Also, it's a thrill to discover that she recognizes literally hundreds of people: high school chums at the coffee shops, college coaches, even secretaries from the languages department at the University of Arizona. They all know Rachel, and she knows all of them, by name. She schedules (we schedule) dates with an array of old pals who come to the house and take her to the mall or the movies or sip tea with her at our kitchen table, putting up with her perseverations like troopers, laughing at her jokes.

But none of this lasts long. I can see the look of weariness on the friends' faces when they return from the mall or café or movie. A look of weariness that tells me that Rachel has been a chore. After such encounters, these friends regard me with new appreciation. "How do you do it?" they seemed to say—or, possibly, "Better you than me."

Even tough-girl Bridget is wearing out. As Rachel's former teammate at the University of Arizona, Bridget has appointed herself Rachel's coach. She lectures, she cajoles. Like most people unfamiliar with brain injury, Bridget believes that Rachel's rehabilitation is a matter of will and determination, like sports.

"Up and at 'em, Rache," she'll say, urging Rachel to walk with the walker or to exercise her right arm.

Rachel does not take this well. She screams at Bridget, bitterly resentful. "You're my fucking friend, not my fucking therapist!"

Bridget comes to me in tears. "I can't take it when Rachel yells at me."

Indeed, resentment is building on both sides, and I am at a loss to mediate it. "Be her friend and not her therapist," I advise Bridget weakly. Then, to Rachel: "Bridget loves you. Don't abuse her friendship." But with the short-term memory deficit, my counseling to Rachel might just as well fall on deaf ears.

Also, I had to remind myself that beautiful Bridget, brimming with good health, svelte and muscled, waving a breezy good-bye to us before her eight-mile "jog" around the neighborhood, must be a constant reminder to Rachel of all she has lost. Indeed, we are interminably caught between the hard rocks of one kind of memory or another—either too much, too little, or too painful.

I've discovered, interestingly, that Rachel will hold onto the memory with the most emotional charge. Not exactly the *memory*, which would involve a recall of precise circumstances, but the *feeling content,* which lingers obsessively. That is to say, that while Rachel forgets the event of my words, she holds fiercely to her feeling of resentment toward Bridget. Weeks after we've discussed a problem, she'll return to it, its emotional vestige still very much alive for her: "She thinks she's my fucking therapist," she grumbles. And I explain that we've worked through that, that Bridget has worked through that, and so on. More and more these days, I find myself becoming short with Rachel. "I've told you that about fifty times," I say hyperbolically, not bothering to disguise the impatient edge in my voice. In fact, I rationalize, that impatient edge might take hold where a calm discussion would fly by. (I have taken to envisioning memory making as a kind of sport fishing: casting the rod to which is attached the perfect lure and then waiting for the random bite.)

When Margot, Steve, and the kids return to their Tucson home for the summer, I am hopeful that Margot will reestablish her sisterly bond with Rachel, that Nick and Maddy will engage Rachel as they used to. In this, I will be disappointed. Margot has her hands full with the kids, and the kids have their hands full with summer activities. Moreover, Rachel has lately become gripped with an extreme, almost pathological restlessness. So when we visit Margot, or anyone for that matter, she becomes frustrated and bored, wanting to leave as soon as we arrive, unable to sit still or to focus on a conversation. Most of these difficulties, I reason, must spring from the short-term memory deficit. For if a person cannot hold in mind the events that fill up each five-minute segment, the sensation must be extreme agitation—boredom, maybe, cranked to its highest and most unendurable pitch.

Moreover, I am beginning to suspect that the fact of her sister is too painful for Margot to bear. It is clear now that the old Rachel will not emerge anytime soon. Once after a short visit to Margot's—Rachel went on her own steam in her walker—she returns home disconsolate. "Margot's way of dealing with me is to park me in front of the TV and give me a bowl of ice cream," she reports unhappily. (Is this true? How does she remember?) In fact, it isn't a bad strategy, though Rachel has little patience with TV and the bowl of ice cream is already contributing to what will become a problem down the line: weight gain.

The ice cream—or more usually the "fro-yo"—is a routine by now. After dinner, we venture out and Rachel orders her usual concoction of flavors, giant size. How can I deny her one of the few pleasures she has left? (What are the others? Snuggling with me and wisecracking with strangers, I suppose.) After fro-yo, Bridget and I turn on TV and "veg," as the saying goes, both worn out by a day or even an evening of Rachel duty. Rachel does not veg; she usually chooses this time to perform her nightly ablutions, which have always been elaborate and ritualistic, in the bathroom.

One evening, already scrubbed and shiny, she makes her way to where we have collapsed on the rattan sofa in the Saltillo-tiled room. We are watching some kind of TV news show which features a young woman who's been separated for years from her mother. Rachel is uncharacteristically focused on this show, and when I look at her face to check for signs of real interest, her eyes are full of tears. "I can't take this story," she says. "It's too sad." Then she clumps into her bedroom, still teary about the mother-daughter separation.

"But they get re-united!" I say, following her. "There's a happy ending!"

Rachel is inconsolable. "It's too sad," she says, shoulders shaking. "This is why I can't take TV."

Another piece of the puzzle? I rack my mind for theories of depression and avoidance—always on the move, hence running away from self? Not for the first time, I think that Rachel would benefit from some kind of therapy and, possibly, from an antidepressant. I am hopeful that her new rehab program at Mirabell will provide some solution.

Mirabell is one of those generic rehab programs located in a generic-looking redbrick building surrounded by purple-blooming Texas rangers and neatly planted cacti. Like Denver, like South Davis. It occurs to me that we might spend our lives rehabbing in such places, among tasteful but commonplace shrubbery, pacing the vinyl floors, sitting on orange plastic chairs, waiting for the intake person to call Rachel's name. Rachel will attend Mirabell five days a week, from nine to two, and will be picked up and dropped off by a driver (thank god, since the treatment center is out of my demonic driving range). She will participate in physical, occupational, and speech therapy and will join a brain injury therapy group headed by a skilled neuropsychologist, Dr. Bach.

I visit at least once a week to check the progress on all fronts. When there, Rachel seems happy enough, joking with the therapists, marching dutifully from station to station. But once home, she complains. "Fucking therapy," she calls it. There is a way in which she feels she doesn't need therapy, that it isn't doing her any good, and she becomes easily frustrated, even enraged. Group therapy especially angers her; she hates, as she puts it, "to be grouped with the brain injured." "They're all lame-asses," she says unkindly.

Dr. Bach, an impeccably dressed man with pale blue, intelligent eyes and a keen understanding of brain injury, reports otherwise. We meet, for the first time, in his modest office in Mirabell and he motions me to a seat. Unlike the other doctors of my experience, he steps around from his desk and takes the chair facing mine.

"How are you dealing with all this?" he asks. I think it is the first time any medical person has asked me that question, and I have to fight my tears of gratitude. "I have a lot of faith in Rachel," I blurt out, but the tears come anyway, in a slow parade down my cheeks.

"It's very hard," he says, and he hands me his own soft white handkerchief. Then he tells me that Rachel is delightful in group therapy, that her wit and intelligence and compassion seem to draw people out.

"At home she behaves like a cranky old woman, always complaining," I say.

"That's about right," he tells me, not without sympathy. "That's the way they all are."

Then there was the day the results of the neuropsych tests arrived from Salt Lake. A fifteen-page document full of fine print and depressing information. I lay on my bed and tried to digest it. It began with a narrative that went something like this: *Rachel Brennan is a 26 year old woman with an exceptional pre-morbid profile, who suffered a severe traumatic brain injury and now shows severe cognitive, emotional and physical limitations.* Of course, she'd royally flunked all the memory tests, but abstract thinking, math skills, even her left-handed grip were also way below average. The only score which managed to creep into average range was reading: Although comprehension was a question mark, due to the memory problems, she apparently read on a twelfth-grade level. Even vocabulary (a surprise, considering Rachel's bouts of eloquence) was considered problematic.

I consoled myself with the fact that Rachel had never been a good standardized test taker. I remembered trying to tutor her for the SATs, and her anxiety level was so high, even in a private session with her mom, that we got nowhere. "She hates tests," I'd explained to the Salt Lake neuropsychologist. He'd nodded politely. After all, what's a little test anxiety in the face of those severe limitations that he would surely find?

I gave a copy of the test results to Dr. Bach, who told me it was about what he'd expected. After that, I shoved the fifteen pages in a file drawer and never read them again.

IT WAS BECOMING CLEAR that our year in Tucson would not put an end to our nightmare (how could I have thought so?), but provide an elaborate unfolding of it. Where the early days of recovery presented a generic picture of severe brain injury—spastic paralysis, perseveration, cognitive impairment of one kind or another—now that we had hunkered down into the routine of post-crisis, post-coma, we'd uncovered an individual picture, like that of Dorian Gray, full of particular grotesqueries. Excruciatingly specific deficits were beginning to pull away from the hazy possibility of a few months ago and establish themselves like chickweed.

I used to lie in bed, the scraggly Queen's palm brushing the screen of my window, and enumerate: the right arm, useless, she carried it in an imaginary sling at her waist, hand clawed and prone to spasm; ditto the wayward (because spastic) right eye; whereas, thanks to therapy, to serial casting, botox, and her sheer will to be on her feet, the right leg was getting strong and purposeful. Perseveration was tapering off, though it still sprang up at times, maddeningly, mostly when she was obsessed with something—a future plan or a phone call from a friend.

When her funny friend Mark called from New York, she talked about it for hours, marveling that they had spoken, wondering when he'd call again, saying over and over and over, "It sure was great to talk to Mark Levin. I sure liked talking to that Mark." Or: "Wasn't it great that Mark called?" Or: "Did I tell you that Mark called?"

"You sure did. That was great that he called. It sounded like you were having a funny conversation."

"Really? What did I say?"

"I didn't really listen, sorry."

"Hey, did I tell you who called me today?"

And the disinhibition was, if anything, more outrageous than before. Or at least it seemed so, since it had taken on a compulsive flavor. She seemed to be addicted to having an audience, craved interaction, perhaps some validation. Possibly, she was determined not to be one of the invisible handicapped, not to be pitied but adored: She spoke cheerfully and intimately to department store clerks, to the preoccupied waiting on grocery store lines, to folks wrapped in privacy in restaurants.

Often, she'd say the same things. Making her way slowly (self-consciously?) through a group of restaurant tables, she'd quip, "Excuse me, I'm so sorry, my right side's on strike" or, more amusingly, "Pardon the madness." Then she'd go into a rambling account of her accident, her previous life as a runner and so on and so forth. I was her stony-faced straight man, urging her onward through the restaurant or grocery store line or department store. And whoever it was would smile politely, frequently compassionate enough to interact with Rachel, prolonging my misery.

At Uma's wedding, Rachel, the maid of honor, was in her element. Uma had asked her to make a speech at the ceremony, which was held in the tree-and-rock-filled setting of Sabino Canyon. Rachel delighted the guests with her speech, which began, *I'm so glad little Uma is finally getting married . . .*

At home, this overfriendly "delightful" girl would decompose into agitation, depression, and, more and more frequently, rage. She had, to put it mildly, a short fuse. If the milk carton slipped from her hand, she would go into paroxysms of anger and frustration, berating herself, berating the injury and fucking Tim C———.

Eventually, Bridget announced she was moving out. "I just can't take Rachel's attitude toward me," she told me, close to tears. I had to remind myself that Bridget was grieving too. She had lost her best friend, whereas I still had my daughter; the difference between motherhood and friendship was right here, at the nexus of personality change. Rachel would always be my daughter—indeed, in her helplessness, she was more my daughter than ever.

Friendship was at once simpler and more complicated: Friends come and go, and yet the richest and most long-lived friendships are dependent on an interaction of sensibilities, on a give-and-take that Rachel was no longer able to participate in. Put Rachel and Bridget together without me, Rachel was sure to fly into a rage, swearing, calling Bridget names, and then Bridget would report all the details I'd just as soon not hear because I would feel responsible, as if some flaw in Rachel's upbringing were finally asserting itself. All the same, it was sad to see Bridget go; for a few months, I'd felt genuinely relieved by her presence, as if Rachel were a burden I'd slipped off one shoulder.

With me, Rachel was kinder. I was rarely the target of her anger, though I was its constant witness. I'd talk her down; then five minutes later she'd be at it again. WHY DID THIS HAPPEN TO ME I WANT TO DIE I'M GOING TO COMMIT SUICIDE. It was as though the perseveration had found a new form in a loop of anger or sorrow. I began to lose patience.

"You have to stop screaming, Rachel," I'd say when I'd reached my limit. "You've got to control yourself or I'll take you to the emergency room and they'll sedate you." This last was not a vain threat; I'd actually considered it. Because how, for hours on end, could a person scream at the top of her lungs—lungs which had resumed their former heft—without doing damage to herself? And how much longer could I endure it? In my darkest moments, I envisioned putting each of us out of our miseries, curling up on the bed with Rachel and drifting quietly off in each other's arms. I astonish myself with this admission, but it's true. But I lack the courage and, more important, the *certainty* for such an act. In the end, I'd usually go to my room and put a pillow over my head and pretend the screams were a distant cat or someone else's baby; and then, when I'd gotten my wits about me, I'd go about talking her down again.

"Just leave the house," advised one well-meaning doctor, when I reported these fits of anger. Easy for him to say. Because how could a mother leave a daughter who was threatening suicide, even if these were frivolous threats? I couldn't do it. Nor could I, for quite some time, manage to convince anyone that she needed medication—antidepressants, anything.

But if the anger was a horror, her restlessness was even more exhausting. No sooner would we return from an outing—a friend's house, a trip to the mall or Bentley's House of Coffee and Tea—than she'd want to know what was next on the agenda. Unlike most brain injured, Rachel seemed never to tire during the day and, also uncharacteristically, slept like a bear all night long. I suppose this was a blessing, but it was unnerving to a person like me, who spent her life lolling on the sofa with a book or parked behind a computer working on a story or poem. At the end of a day crammed, to my mind, with activity, Rachel would complain that we'd done nothing, that she was bored out of her mind. She couldn't focus enough to watch TV or read; she couldn't even hang out at a dinner table without jumping up and down to carry dishes one-handed, in either her wheelchair or her walker, to the sink, scraping and stacking, as if she were still a waitress at Bentley's. Nor could she sustain any kind of conversation. When the talk strayed from matters Rachel—she relished all talk of her injury and recovery as well as being the comic center of any gathering—she became disconsolate, aggressively bored, sighing loudly, shooting me dark looks across the table.

I was at a loss. On one hand, I wanted her to be included and could understand her desolation and frustration when the conversation moved too fast for her; but on the other, I felt an obligation to socialize her, to make her fit for a dinner table full of friends. I made an effort to ignore, therefore, those dark looks aimed in my direction, but it wasn't long before the dishes were piled on her walker shelf and she'd be noisily—and perhaps, passive aggressively—off, clanking pot against plate, and running the water so loudly our guests had to shout to hear each other.

I tried to imagine what it was like for Rachel, going through life in a blur, hedging her bets against the poor odds of her remembering: a kind of skilled balancing act, I supposed, between what she knew and what she thought she should know. Most of her energy seemed to go toward coping strategies, trying to appear normal—witty, smart, observant—as well as covering up the short-term memory failure by expert deductions from whatever evidence happened to be handy. Memory, I'd come to believe, is an act of imagining what has past. Or deducing.

Her afternoon at the mall with Karen Sahn is an example. For hours, Karen pushed her from Banana Republic to Ann Taylor to the Gap. I'm sure Rachel was in heaven, but when she came home she was barely able to recall her outing. She deduced that she had spent some money—the Gap shopping bag, the crumpled receipt in her backpack. But as evening wore on, the details of her day faded from her mind, much like the dark blueness descending over the spectacular sunset we were having. I knew her personal nightfall was coming when she answered each question with an interrogatory.

"Where did you go today, Rachel?"

"To the mall with Sahnny?"

"Right. Did you buy anything?"

"Maybe a couple of shirts?"

"What do they look like?"

"One is brown with white and blue and black stripes, a zipper and short sleeves."

"Are you looking at it?" (I had moved to the kitchen and was disengaging her receipts from their cranky bundle at the bottom of her pack.)

"Totally!"

I was also experiencing first-hand how a poor short-term memory affects a person's sense of time passing. Rachel seemed to have no patience whatsoever. One morning, she almost went mad waiting for Uma to come and take her for breakfast. She checked her watch compulsively, scooted to the door and back again to the bedroom, where I sat behind my computer, fiddling with a poem. Under the best of circumstances, Uma, in the throes of an intense dermatological residency, was a half hour late, but today it was an hour that felt like days. When she finally arrived, Rachel was purple with rage and frustration, hysterical. And I was almost as bad. "We HAVE been waiting," I told Uma, who looked a little taken aback.

But here we were in Tucson, where on any outing Rachel would run into someone she knew from the past. And if she didn't quite know them, she'd pretend she did, patting them one-handed on the arm, greeting them joyously. People would join us at tables in restaurants, jot down our number, make dates with Rachel (which she'd promptly forget), seem on the whole delighted to see her. After such encounters she seemed to remember the flavor of the day—happy or annoying—but she couldn't fill in the details that gave it a deeper meaning.

"So what did we do today, Rachel?" I'd ask, and she'd look blank. "Name just one thing," I'd persist.

"Hmmm," she'd say, and then she'd make a wild guess which, depending on her mood, was either reasonable or wacky. "Let's see, didn't we rob a bank or something, Girlfriend?" Very pleased with herself.

Even cueing didn't help much in those days. "We ran into someone in the mall who has blond hair who you know from college." No idea. "We ran into someone in the mall who wants you to go to the movies next week."

"I hate the fucking movies, Girlfriend."

"That may be, but you made this date with so-and-so."

"My memory must really suck."

"Why don't you write things down?"

"BECAUSE MY FUCKING HAND DOESN'T WORK THAT'S WHY. Oh, sorry, Girlfriend."

The handwriting stuff was only partially true, since her left-handed penmanship was becoming quite readable. She kept a small journal of rants—things like, *my fucking life sucks, why do I have to live like this?* over and over—and she loved it when I gave her writing assignments. I parked her at Bentley's with a large budget for iced mochas one afternoon and she worked away. The assignment: write a funny story about anyone who sits nearby. *Abe is obsessed with numerals, whereas Jane has many kittens. His balding head does not appeal to her, therefore.* She still couldn't seem to put her characters into action, but she did write some quirky and vivid character sketches. (This made me wonder, not for the first time, about the connection between the brain, memory, and narrative strengths and weaknesses . . .)

She resisted writing down events or engagements—the purpose seemed to elude her. She felt she could remember most things when, in fact, she seldom remembered anything at all. In late spring, we went to the Street Fair in Tucson, a biannual event that drew thousands of people. We brought the wheelchair so that Rachel could propel herself one-footed, rather than try to make her laborious way in the walker. Within minutes, Rachel had disappeared into the vast crowd, and Bridget and I were scouring Fourth Avenue for her. It didn't help that she was in the waist-high chair, not easily visible either through the bodies or over the heads of the fair-goers. I counted on her acute hearing—indeed, post-injury, Rachel could hear a pin drop in a restaurant—but even calling her name, *Rachel! Rachel!*, as if I were calling my puppy, was futile on this occasion. Fourth Avenue was a sea of shoppers, carnival acts, musicians, vendors, teenagers, toddlers, and parents, and Rachel, whose nose could have led her anywhere, was not to be found.

Bridget and I split up and began asking people—girl in a wheelchair? Very friendly? We had no doubt that, even in this crowd, Rachel would make herself noticed. After about an hour, which felt like five hours, someone directed me to a booth where Rachel was busily negotiating with the vendor for a ponyskin handbag. In fact, he let her have it for half price, since she didn't have full price on her. The bag, it turned out, was for me: "A present for my girlfriend who has stuck by me through thick and thin."

But I'd given that money—too much money—to Rachel

for herself: her weekly allowance, part of which I'd thought she might spend at the street fair. I tried to look grateful, feeling vaguely the political incorrectness of that black-and-white pony fur, petting it tentatively, still unnerved by my search for her. This would be the first of many occasions on which Rachel would vanish for long periods of time. I began to say it was my hobby, looking for Rachel, and as time went on my searches became less frantic, more casual. If I closed my eyes, I'd sometimes imagine I saw her, and then I'd head to that place and there she'd be. Mostly I wasn't that lucky. Mostly, I'd simply wander, following my own nose, and eventually she'd turn up—at a frozen yogurt counter or a shoe store or trudging around the corner, a bagel and an iced latté balanced on the shelf of her walker. As soon as she could walk, she seized her independence, and I have to say I gave her free reign. Though it wasn't always safe: I knew this. But some instinct told me that if Rachel were to evolve at all, she must be allowed her freedom to explore the world, as precarious as that freedom might turn out to be.

"Where were you, Rachel?" I'd say after one of these disappearing acts.

Rachel, who had perfected the rueful smile—a little guilty, a little amused—would say, "Who knows?"

The two of us used to laugh about it. We made up a phrase that might have been the title for something, if only we knew what its content was: *The Secret Life of Rachel Brennan, Unknown Even to Herself.*

For example, after the street fair outing, Rachel received a visit from an old high school friend, Paul, whom she'd apparently arranged to meet. Paul, sandy-haired, attractive, with a wide friendly smile, was obviously pleased to see Rachel. He gave her a warm hug, which she returned with some ardor.

"How did you know where to find us?" I asked, curious to know if Rachel had actually remembered our address.

"I looked in her purse," Paul said cheerfully. Oh right, I thought—weeks ago, when she first began to travel on her own steam, I'd tucked a card with her name, address, and phone number in her purse.

"Did you remember meeting Paul at the fair?" I asked Rachel later.

"Not even," she said with a laugh.

Nevertheless, when I was attending my Warren Wilson residency a few weeks later, Rachel apparently—I say *apparently* because here we have a stunning example of her secret life—had a fling with Paul. Bridget, who valiantly offered to live with Rachel during my ten-day stay in North Carolina, reported that one night she didn't come home from a date with Paul. The next day, Bridget found Rachel and Paul in Bentley's, Rachel looking flushed and happy, Paul looking somewhat chagrined. But whatever their connection, it terminated not long after my return from Warren Wilson. I'm sure Rachel's inappropriateness was a factor, among other things. I overheard her on the phone to him one afternoon, repeating herself: "So when do I get to see you? So when do I get to see you?" Then, after a few more minutes: "So when do I get to see you?" Paul—who could blame him?—slipped quietly out of the picture, and Rachel, who'd, perhaps fortunately, already forgotten this brief romantic episode in her post-injury life, was not devastated.

The speech therapist, a budding playwright, tried to cajole Rachel into using a day planner, which, sadly, she resisted with her very soul. Otherwise she adored Jay, who got her jokes, who seemed genuinely fond of her. In another life, they might have been best friends (I was always playing this trick of before and after with myself, though it was a torment to imagine what might have been, what should have been). Jay was outrageously gay with punked-out blond hair and a lot of energy, as well as the prerequisite speech-therapy patience.

Besides buying her a purple day timer, Jay worked with Rachel on writing stories about her day and jotting down "feeling" entries in her journal. The former were always oddball inventions, compensations for a memory not there, while the latter oscillated between two channels, pure misery or, to use a Rachel neologism, good sportitude. These attempts to bolster herself I find most wrenching, betraying her struggle for insight and her failure to find it.

A wave of negativity just now hit me. I frequently find myself thinking why me? Why me? I allow myself to go on a roller coaster ride with negativity. I can now think only negative thoughts. But I know this accident's repercussions could have been a lot worse. I mean I could have lost both legs. And hospital workers would shake their heads and talk among themselves and say, "And she used to be a University runner."

"Why *didn't* God just take me?" she once asked in a reflective moment. We were lying in her bed, our arms around each other.

"I don't know, Rache," I said. "Maybe he has a plan for you, something you're supposed to do with your life." I was thinking of the notion of karma: burning it up in one life so that the next will be easier or more spiritual or something.

"I think he saved me so I could keep you company," she said, snuggling closer. "I think he didn't want you to be alone."

WE TOOK SEVERAL trips in the summer and fall of 1996. In late August, we went to Alamos, Mexico, to visit my childhood friend Sue, who owns a hotel in this charming colonial city. Rachel was in her element, speaking Spanish with the hotel staff, cruising the hallways in her fancy walker, exchanging salsa CDs with an especially jovial taxi driver named Bruno. We were surrounded by old friends, people I hadn't seen in years, and it seemed to me as we sat beneath the Mexican sky, listening to the chatter of Sonoran birds, that Rachel and I had arrived somewhere safe again.

Though the worst thing that's been said to me since Rachel's accident was said in Alamos. "When I talk to Rachel," said a friend, meaning to empathize, "I'm not sure if anyone's *in there*." The friend and I had been drinking margaritas, and Rachel had been talking to a waiter in her animated way. It had been a beautiful night, the air had that clarity and depth that mark the end of a day of great weather, and around us the little glass-covered candles on the patio flickered romantically. I had been having a euphoric time until the well-meaning friend made his remark. Really, I was astonished as much as hurt. Because look at her over there, talking to the waiter, using her one good hand to gesture, to joke, making him laugh, comforting him with her trademark *pat pat* on the shoulder, listening with her face alert, smiling. Surely, for the waiter, someone was *in there*.

The next day, for example, we met a wonderful priest

there, too, a Father Charles, who took us to see a young man named Manuel. Manuel, disabled in a car accident, was bedridden. He lived in a small cement-block house with his mother, who tended to him. To pass the time, he fashioned purses out of cigarette packs. In Manuel's presence, Rachel changed from the somewhat narcissistic brain injured girl to a compassionate friend. Settling herself at the foot of his bed, she spoke and listened patiently, her whole demeanor becoming softer and oddly more focused. She came away from Manuel's bedside with a free purse and with some insight into her own relatively lucky condition. "I think I should count my blessings," she said soberly.

The other trip was in November for the occasion of my mother's eightieth birthday in Florida. This would be the first time my parents would see the new Rachel, and I worried about the shock it might cause them. On the long plane ride, Rachel had been difficult: anxiety-ridden, angry, restless. But once at my parents' home in Delray Beach, she shifted into entertainment mode, "girlfriending" all the senior citizens, who tittered nervously in response. My mother had been most concerned about Rachel's dormant right arm and hand. "Make her use it more," she admonished. It was true; the right arm and hand might as well not have existed. Rachel lacked the patience to try the simplest things. "Tear off a hunk of bread, hold a cup," Deb Wagner had advised. But with so many other deficits to improve, the right arm seemed the least of it. The fingers were absolutely paralyzed into a shell-like curve, though she was able, with great difficulty, to open her hand and close it again, which was more than Mom could do.

It was strange to be there in Delray, flanked by my disabled mother and daughter. I was going to say it was like déjà vu, but that wouldn't be quite accurate. In the early Salt Lake days, when Rachel had first come home from the hospital, when we were still sharing my bed, she confided to me that she had always known this would happen to her. Whether that certainty came from an errant memory loop or not, I realized in that moment that I had always known it, too. Somewhere, in some obscure layer of consciousness and prescience, I had known all of it. And so had she. Maybe this is why I spurred her on in her pre-accident adventures. The pre-injury Rachel had to cram all that experience into twenty-five years. And she'd done it.

THE ONE-YEAR ANNIVERSARY of the accident came and went. August 17: It's just a day, I told myself, and so it turned out to be just a day. We did the ordinary things—therapy, meals—and I kept those flashes of my own memory under control. I was turning into a person who persisted despite the odds, "who did not break down in [my] lines and weep," as Yeats's poem "Lapis Lazuli" goes. In fact, I rarely wept. Sometimes I felt the tears gathering themselves, like unarticulated words, off in a distant part of me, but, except on rare occasions, I knew I could not afford to give them credence.

Two and a half weeks later, on September 5, we celebrated Rachel's twenty-sixth birthday. I shopped for groceries and made a few cakes and invited about thirty friends, including Margot, Steve, and the kids, the father figures John and Tom, Auntie Mary Pat and Uncle Peter. Looking back on the occasion, I see myself going through the motions with a kind of driven dutifulness, but without much joy. Rachel held court, shocking and amusing the guests with her disinhibited wisecracks. "She is so delightful!" someone whispered to me. My friend Barbara Anderson humorously observed that Rachel was exactly as she used to be after two gin and tonics. "And I remember Rachel after two gin and tonics," she said. But the jokes, for me, were beginning to wear thin.

Dear Sweet Diary: I feel as though I'm waking up from a bad dream because I mean I don't know the difference between right or left. I mean I do, but I'm trying to simplify everything . . .
— Rachel's journal, 1997

To TEST THE REALITY of Rachel's complaints about Mirabell, which continued unabated as the weeks went by, I decided to accompany her to a full day of therapy.

We were picked up by Pablo in the big van. Rachel had made friends with Pablo; with him she was able to practice her Spanish. That day she and Pablo sang Spanish songs. Pablo would start one and Rachel would follow in her happy, toneless voice (she had always been tone-deaf) or she'd start and Pablo would chime in. The sounds of their voices filled the van as we chugged down Grant Road to the treatment center. I was relieved to be a nonparticipant, watching the view go by. I had a toothache and was not in the mood for conversation, and I was grateful that Rachel's people skills were in full gear that morning.

One of the reasons I'd decided to accompany her for the day was Phil. Recently, Rachel had been given a ledger in which she taped photographs of her therapists. Because her recall for people and images was so good, she'd been able to tell me about each person. Phil was the therapist she disliked. When she mentioned Phil, her face clouded over. "He's so uptight; he has no compassion for the handicapped." On the days when she came home most shaken and upset, I knew she'd spent time with Phil. At the start of the day, I saw from Rachel's day planner, she had two sessions scheduled with Phil.

We were a bit early, and we saw Phil pass by once or twice looking harried. He shuffled papers around in a file as if he'd lost something, then glanced around the room of waiting clients and a few caregivers, not greeting any of us. Sitting nearby were Marcia and her mother, Joan. Marcia, a thirty-something woman with a wide smile, was in a wheelchair (as opposed to Rachel's walker) and spoke overloudly, overenthusiastically, in the way of the head injured. Rachel, who was also prone to these behaviors, leaned over and whispered *sotto voce,* "At least I can thank my lucky stars I'm not like *that*." Marcia's mother and I exchanged amused glances.

Phil finally appeared and wordlessly beckoned to us. He was a small, attractive Hispanic man with dark hair that had a sprinkling of gray across the top, almost as if he'd passed under a light snow flurry. He struck me as quite serious, perhaps a bit melancholy. I accompanied him and Rachel into a treatment room where he would work with her on some speech therapy. Technically, Phil was an aide, not a bona fide therapist. He filled in when Jay or the other therapists were busy elsewhere. In this day of managed care, Phil was the person who saw Rachel most frequently. Today, Jay had given him an assignment to work through with Rachel: create a lesson plan for teaching hospital volunteers some necessary Spanish phrases.

Rachel began by writing the heading GREETINGS across the page. Then she wrote three or four Spanish greetings: *Hola, que tal? Como estas? Buenas Dias.* Her left-handed writing was labored and almost illegible. I could tell she was getting frustrated. Phil wasn't lively or encouraging. He made poorly timed suggestions.

"What if, for example, someone wants to know how to get someplace?" he prompted. But Rachel was still on "greetings." When she suggested conjugating verbs, he laughed. It was not a good match. Phil was well-meaning but insensitive to Rachel's points of frustration. She managed, nonetheless, to cover an entire page with Spanish phrases hospital volunteers might want to know. She simplified Phil's suggestion about directions by writing the words for "right," "left," "straight," and so on. She was bored. She was scowling. Her handwriting was decomposing as her concentration diminished. When Phil stepped out of the room, she made a face.

"I'm not a moron," she said. "This is very elementary. Doesn't he believe I know Spanish?" For her, the exercise had turned into a test; moreover, she seemed to have forgotten its point.

After this, Rachel and Phil walked the corridors, she with an aluminum four-pronged cane. She did brilliantly. Her balance and gait, though painstakingly slow, were steady.

After the workout, she asked Phil if he thought her athleti-cism had contributed to her good recovery. "You are not recovering as well as you were at first," he said. "Now you have plateaued." Her face fell, as if a curtain had dropped. Furious, I made a note to talk to Jay about Phil.

Next on the agenda was brain injury group with Dr. Bach, and, since I was not invited to this meeting, I went out-side. I stood by the cactus Xeriscape in front of the rehab building and let the heat warm my toothache-y face. I was still trembling from Phil's tactlessness when Joan, the mother of Marcia, spied me.

"I wanted to introduce myself," she said. She looked incredibly tired. She was neatly dressed in a denim skirt and a flowered blouse, her tan hair pulled back in a ponytail. But her cheeks were slack, hopeless. She wore square-framed glasses, the kind sold at Walgreens, and behind them her eyes appeared to be the same color as her hair, a nondescript beige. I describe her not to be cruel, but to convey that her appearance somehow suggested all that she had been through with her daughter's recovery. Time had worn her down to one color.

She told me that Marcia had been in a coma for seven months and that, like Rachel, she had been a University of Arizona student. She said it had been six years since her daughter's accident and that insurance was very hard.

"I guess you haven't run into that yet," she said. I said I hadn't, really. She nodded. "We read about Rachel in the paper last year, and we thought, oh no, there's another one."

Our conversation was gloomy out there amid the aloes and the purple blooms of the Texas ranger. A light breeze blew softly but so steadily that the fabric of Joan's blouse trembled as if it were being propelled by a tiny machine. At one point, she reached up to her eye and wiped a tear.

It wasn't long after that that Rachel's Mirabell therapy was cut back and, finally, stopped altogether. Like a bad high school kid, she was more or less expelled. Pablo, the amiable driver, had begun complaining about her. When he arrived to pick her up, he had to wait too long. This was more or less true. Pablo's arrivals spanned a period of twenty minutes, one way or another, around the appointed hour, and no sooner would Rachel be on the porch waiting for the van's arrival, then she'd have to pee. This was a slow process: re-entering the house and slowly maneuvering her walker down the hall and into the bathroom; and next, the struggle with clothing, the inevitable waiting for the pee that was often no more than a trickle, the washing of hands. Invariably, Pablo would arrive somewhere in the middle of this operation and be kept waiting.

I tried to explain this to the Mirabell administrator, a pretty brunette who was wheelchair-bound herself, but I couldn't seem to convince her that Rachel's lateness was not due simply to time management problems on Rachel's part and lack of consideration on mine. She added that Rachel seemed resistant to therapy as well. Of this I had no doubt. Rachel's denial was immense; she seemed to think all she needed were some hard workouts, not the slow, enigmatic manipulations of the neurophysical therapists. Plus, hanging around with the brain injured on a daily basis seemed only to reinforce her worst fears about herself.

The gap between who she had been and who she now was must have been deeply elusive to her, as if her old and new selves were marooned on two different islands. She thought she still inhabited her old self, but when she rummaged around for a familiar landmark, it was no longer available. The deepest and most mysterious effect of a severe brain injury, it seems to me, must be this: the absence of the self—an organic (rather than psychological) identity problem. How to deal with this new strange self and its weird behavioral and cognitive characteristics? How to imagine being someone you're not?

Pablo's other complaint, possibly more serious as well as more laughable, was the matter of Rachel's language, which offended him. Her propensity to utter whatever came to mind revealed, mostly, her sweet and humorous nature. But she was also a wiseass, given to irreverent and, frequently, obscene cracks whenever the spirit moved her. And even though obscenity is commonplace in brain injured patients, she was out on her ear, my disinhibited daughter with her unruly brain and her bad short-term memory, and we were left to our own devices. Which felt slim to me.

I, the caregiver, was wearing out. In the mornings I awoke with a feeling of dread—awakening not *from* a nightmare but *to* the nightmare of our real lives. I could feel the dread—there's no other word for this palled feeling—as if the shroud of reality were slowly creeping across my body, as if only in dreams could I return to our former, carefree existence. In the bathroom, Rachel would be well into her rituals—water running, teeth brushing, toilet flushing—and this would momentarily comfort me. I'd remember, then, that there would be no therapy, there would be no family coming to call.

Margot and Steve had left for the new basketball season in Chicago; my sister was busy with her decorating business;

even my pals, Beth and Robin, had lives, after all. And John, whose attention and love meant so much to us, had become involved with a new woman and so was unavailable too.

Moreover, Rachel's father, Tom, whose school-bus dwelling was twenty minutes away, came infrequently, on the odd Saturday. (I should mention that none of us have been invited to his school bus, and so we are left with our fantasies of it, surrounded by old car parts and rusting fenders, the dog Buster lounging nearby, breathing laboriously through his nostrils in the desert heat.) Time with Rachel seemed to wear Tom out, too. Once he arrived with a weird gift—a pair of shoes he'd purchased at the swap meet, a full size too small for Rachel. They were brown boots, at least fifteen years old, with little scenes hand-painted on the tops, below the laces, and were charming in their way. Rachel, much more conservative in her tastes than her funky parents, had nothing but contempt for these shoes. "And, to top it all off," she exclaimed later, and on many occasions thereafter, "they're too small!" Unreasonably, Tom seemed hurt that Rachel refused to wear them. (Hello Tom? She's got a spastic right foot!)

One of our more amusing moments came with Tom, however. Since no one has actually seen the school bus he lives in somewhere outside Green Valley—he makes a point of telling us there are actually *two* school buses, not *one*—I told him one evening I had trouble visualizing it all. So he made a tiny, complicated drawing on a paper napkin. A school bus joined vertically to another school bus on top of which was insanely perched the shell of an old VW. The more he drew, the more absurd it seemed, beyond Rube Goldberg, and as the drawing increased in complexity—

shaky lines for plumbing, a makeshift shower area, little squares for sleep and cooking—it became even harder to visualize than before he put ballpoint to napkin. "And then," he said, almost a non sequitur, "the pack rats invaded and chewed up everything." Rachel and I locked eyes and, almost in unison, rolled them. And in a fine achievement of self-control, Rachel kept back her laughter. Instead she remarked slyly, "Good Lord."

So we saw everyone once in a while, but it wasn't enough for me. Mostly I felt abandoned, lonely. Whereas, in the beginning, I was spurred to action on Rachel's behalf, now all will seemed to leave my body. It became clear that no one would be there for Rachel but me, and a kind of resigned lethargy took hold. When friends and family finally called for a short visit, it was all I could do to drag myself from the bedroom to see them.

I remember talking long-distance to my old grad school friend Cynthia Hogue, complaining bitterly that I needed someone to help me. "If only," I'd said, "there was one person who would agree to take this on with me." Cynthia listened sympathetically, then insightfully observed, "You need Rachel." The old Rachel is who Cynthia was thinking of—because the old Rachel would have been there for us, whoever we were.

I recounted this to Dr. Bach, who had agreed to take Rachel and me as separate clients at his elegant home office in the Tucson foothills. "You have lost a great deal," Dr. Bach said. Yes, I thought sorrowfully, I have lost everything. From outside his office window, I could hear the mourning doves and see the pale blue February sky, blithely prevailing despite our sufferings. The whole world seemed unfair in that moment, and I didn't want Dr. Bach to agree with me. I wanted a little injection of hope. Even delusion. Instead, he flipped through his DSM-IV and pronounced me to be in a major depression. He gave me the name of a psychiatrist who would be able to prescribe medication.

For her part, Rachel's time with Dr. Bach seemed happier. She appeared quite joyous after her sessions with him (there were about four sessions in all), and I was surprised the day that he recommended that she terminate. "Her memory is such that she can't carry through from one session to the next," he told me. That was the same day I had reported to Dr. Bach that Rachel remembered him and his wife, that she was able to describe their home in considerable detail. "But what good is it all if she can't remember events?" he'd asked me. So Rachel and I trundled off to the psychiatrist, hoping for reprieve.

The psychiatrist, Dr. Gray, I was surprised to discover, was a meditator. Posters depicting the Tibetan Buddha adorned the walls of his office and were an enormous comfort to me—I suppose the notion that a medical doctor also had a spiritual life indicated that he would not be one of the False Hope Cops. Which, in fact, he wasn't. Without hesitation, he put Rachel on a drug regime which she's continued, more or less, to this day. "She has," he told me after I recounted her growing hysterias, "an organic mood disorder." As a result of her accident, Rachel's brain chemistry is off-kilter, causing, among other things, imbalances in serotonin levels. He began her on the antidepressant Zoloft, a serotonin re-uptake inhibitor (SRI), and Depakote, an antiseizure medication which is effective in brain injury mood disorder.

Almost immediately these drugs worked. Rachel's mood

swings—elation as well as depression and anger—calmed. She seemed altogether more focused and happy, even more energetic. (Me he put on Paxil, a mild SRI that, unfortunately, only made me serene in a lobotomized kind of way and gave me terrible diarrhea. I took it for a month, then decided it was too weird.)

As Rachel's mood improved—no longer those excruciating bouts of anger, screaming, and suicidal threats—so did mine. Like the classic co-dependent, I followed Rachel's lead: I awoke full of hope and plans and new energy. In a later session, Dr. Gray would tell me that I probably didn't need an antidepressant. "On second thought," he admitted, "I would prescribe a mild anti-anxiety for you, if anything."

So we were actually reprieved!

Another form of reprieve came in the form of a gift from Steve: a recumbent stationary bicycle for Rachel. Just the thing for my jock girl. Now that her moods were under control, she reveled in each mile she pedaled. Sometimes she rode for an hour and a half, working up such a sweat that her T-shirt and shorts were soaked right through, as if she'd been pushed into a swimming pool. This aerobic exercise seemed to help her moods as well, filling her with confidence and hope.

"Girlfriend," she'd brag, "I did two whole workouts today—the short three-mile and the longer six-mile!"

"You're a stud," I'd say. "There's no one like Raquelita!"

Indeed, when I tried a few slow, flat miles on her bike, I could pedal for only ten minutes before hoisting myself, wobbly-legged, to a chair. "Just take it slow," she'd advise—this was the old Rachel again, condescending to me—"just be gradual and you'll get there." But, for the record, I never got there on the recumbent bike.

Rachel, on the other hand, grew stronger and stronger. In a few months, her legs would have the heft of tree trunks, and her butt would be as firm as a car hood. And she was happy. That was the main thing. She measured, and still measures, her recovery by her physique. Dr. Bach was impressed. In brain injury, he told me, any challenge helps recovery because it causes those neurons to begin sparking. So physical exercise, as it draws upon the brain's resources, may actually help cognition. What an idea!

Fueled with new hope—the Guadalupe was never far from us, though I give her shorter shrift than she deserves in these pages—I set out to take Rachel to a few new-age health workers. Somewhere, I believed, a cure was lurking, if only we were persistent enough to find it. We began simply, with massage. For $120, I bought a package of four treatments (which I repeatedly renewed) at a new facility, reputed for its expertly trained employees and for the variety of "modalities" offered, which included cranio-sacral and shiatzu. Although Rachel resisted anything faintly resembling therapy, she sourly agreed to the massages, which became part of our weekly regime. After a month, Rachel was standing straighter and walking with a firmer gait in her walker.

Still, she whined about the massages, which seemed to her "a colossal waste of time." I suspect this had more to do with removing her clothes than it did with the massages themselves. Despite the rigor of her daily workouts, she'd gained even more weight since starting the Depakote and Zoloft, and I think she was ashamed of her new body. At her monthly appointments with her Tucson physiatrist, she dreaded getting on the scale. Then she'd perseverate for hours about her weight gain.

Except for his terrible scale, Dr. Cooper, with his tooled-hide cowboy boots and dark, shaggy hair, appealed to Rachel. He applauded her gains—especially on the stationary bike—and was, on the whole, hopeful and encouraging to both of us. Still, after each appointment, Rachel would go on about her weight. "Now I'm a fat chick," she'd say.

Why, out of all the events of her day, would this fact rise insistently from the chaos of her memory? Months ago, I'd tried to puzzle out the differences between making a memory—that is, storing—and retrieving a memory. It seemed to me that Rachel did store memories, possibly all memories of all events. And though the new thinkers on memory have disabused us of the notion that memory is like a computer, to me it seems an apt analogy. Because somewhere amid the vastness of neurons (two billion, we're told) and brain chemicals, those memories got hidden, I was sure, just like a document in Word Perfect gets inadvertently shuffled to a miscellaneous file folder. Retrieval seemed to be Rachel's *bête noire*, her inability to locate a particular memory wherever it had squirreled itself away.

My evidence for this was the eerie fact that the odd memory would surface days after an event, an occurrence that became commonplace for Rachel as time went on. It was shocking really. Sitting in a restaurant, she'd suddenly ask if we were next going to her massage, which in actuality had taken place the day before. Crucially, she had no memory of this event *as past*. Could a short-term memory produce a timewarp? Files again. Is there a minuscule "done" box in the human brain, marking an event as finished?

On the recommendation of a friend, I took Rachel—oh what trepidation, way outside my driving range, and so I trembled for miles up Oracle Road, past the soft desert foothills of the Catalina mountain range, the sun scorching us through the windows of the Nissan, despite air-conditioning—to a man named William, a master acupuncturist and cranio-sacral expert. Cranio-sacral might be the way to go, I reasoned, it being a procedure reputed to have a direct effect on the deep structures of the brain. Cranio-sacral had been a disappointment in Rachel's hospital days, but I felt we owed it another chance.

William, a white-haired, white-bearded giant, who lived on what might be described as a compound with many worshipful assistants (trainees, I believe) milling around, took to Rachel immediately. During the course of a month, ebullient William administered cranio-sacral as well as acupuncture to Rachel. I sat on the sidelines, amusing myself by taking notes for a story in which William would figure as a kind of comic protagonist. Slapping around in rubber thongs and cutoff jean shorts, he was kind of a macho guru, the type of person you could imagine persuading a group of followers to give up their worldly possessions and reside in huts. But he was also, clearly, good-hearted and dedicated.

At the time, I felt the acupuncture was helping Rachel physically. But the small changes she experienced—a tad more mobility in the right leg, a bout of marginally improved memory—might have occurred without William. After a while, we stopped, mainly because of money. At twice a week and seventy-five dollars a session, William's therapies were digging too deeply into our resources.

Around this time, I met Dr. Andrew Weil at a dinner party given for a medical conference I was invited to participate in. I was to deliver part of my seminal essay on Rachel, and Dr. Weil, as national health guru, was the keynote speaker. Though it was against my nature, I managed to muscle my way into a seat next to him, and, as we nibbled on guacamole and chips, I told him about Rachel. In person, he looks much younger and even healthier than he appears on the covers of his highly popular books, and this compelled my confidence. "Well," he said, after listening seriously to my outpourings—the story of Rachel in a minute and a half— "I'd recommend Feldenkreis and Tomatis."

"Excuse me?" I said. I thought he might be referring to the next course.

"She'll be cured," he said, crunching into another chip and beaming at me.

So at Andrew Weil's suggestion, we began a new kind of physical therapy called Feldenkreis. The Feldenkreis therapist, Rich, a mild-mannered, balding man whose office was in his tiny apartment, explained that Feldenkreis, unlike traditional physical therapy, involved the bones rather than the muscles. There was a real skeleton hanging from Rich's ceiling, which was, I suppose, a tribute to this fact. The human skeleton, Rich explained to me, can actually find easier and more natural ways of moving, if given the chance.

The results of Rich's work with Rachel were quite remarkable. Rich would place Rachel, prone or seated, on a massage table and, simply by manipulating her skeleton— adjusting the position of an arm or leg, for example, or turning her torso, he would liberate a whole complex of movements. One day, after some very small adjustments, Rachel actually stood up by herself.

Homework, as a way of reinforcing these routines, was crucial to Feldenkreis, however, and neither Rachel nor I was up to the "homework." She, because she hated it, natch, and me, because I was tired of fighting with her about therapy, much less "homework." Nevertheless, we kept up the Feldenkreis until we returned to Salt Lake.

Tomatis, a therapy involving "listening" to specially modulated tapes through headphones, is based on the theory that the ear organizes all the activities of the brain cells. Tomatis has gained some reputation for miracle cures of dyslexia and other learning difficulties. It's even supposed to help with balance. But it's very costly. Though we drove to Phoenix to investigate one of its centers, we never signed on. Maybe someday.

Without a doubt, Rachel continued to recover. Weekly, we'd see improvements—even though the improvements were subtle and inconsistent. People would comment: "She seems much more aware." Which was true. I saw it in her face, which seemed to be moving toward her former expression, the canniness returning to her eyes and smile. Was that what people noticed? Or was it the change in mood, the effect of the new meds? I could leave her alone for hours now, going about my chores in the library or at the University of Arizona, where, for the spring semester, I taught an undergraduate workshop. Rachel busied herself tidying up the kitchen—years later, someone would dub her "Tidy Spice"—and reading.

One afternoon, I came home to find Rachel reclined on

her bed with a *New Yorker*. Her hair was still wet from the shower she must have taken after one of her monster workouts. "This is a great article," she said, waving the magazine at me. But when I asked her to tell me about it, she realized it was already gone. "Short-term memory," she shrugged with a grin. Still, she persisted with the particular article (the article my long-term memory has failed to retrieve at the moment of this writing), reading the same few paragraphs over and over throughout the course of a few weeks: because she'd forgotten, of course, what she'd read, even though, after a while, she remembered that she'd read it and forgot it. "This is a great article," she'd say, and the cycle would begin again. With the reinforcement her repetitions provided, however, she would eventually glean a sort of topic area from the article, like "something to do with a female athlete?" or "dogs, I think?" Always the question mark at the end of each sentence, underscoring the bewildered nature of her world.

With all our wanderings from therapist to therapist, factoring in time for the physiatrist Dr. Cooper, the bladder experts at the University of Arizona Health Sciences (her bladder *was* spastic; she was put on *ditripan*, which helped), my visits to Dr. Bach, and occasional check-ins with Dr. Gray, our days were full of activity.

But our off-hours were becoming more lighthearted, a genuine break from our daily grind, thanks to a group of friends I had not counted on. These were Jane Miller, her partner Kim Westerman, and Barbara Culley and her partner, Frances Sherberg. I'd been friends with these women, all poets, when I'd lived in Tucson years ago, but we'd not been the kind of friends who called each other daily and shared meals at least once a week. Now we were. Without any hesitation, they welcomed Rachel into their lives, laughing with her, lavishing affection and friendship on both of us. They were a warm balm from heaven, my angel friends, and I still don't know if any of them realizes how absolutely crucial they were to our time in Tucson. Let this be their tribute.

Saturday would find all of us lounging around in our family room, planning a great meal. I remember the night Kim—a truly gifted chef—and I made steaks on the grill, a squash and red pepper soup, and arugula salad with a piquant orange vinaigrette. Dessert may have been crème brûlée. We all clapped at the finish, over a wonderful port. Afterward, dancing around the kitchen, Rachel in my arms, shaking, as she put it, her *bootay*, Jane said, "Those two are beyond incest."

We lived through the most exciting basketball season of Steve's career that spring of 1997, as well as the super success of Lute Olson's University of Arizona Wildcats. Rache and I watched it all with our girlfriends in the family room, the outside din so enormous after the Cats won the championship that when we opened the door, it sounded like a tidal wave was roaring toward us. And Steve, in a moment of great grace and luck, made the winning shot of the Bulls' NBA season, while Rachel and our pals looked on in open-mouthed astonishment. Surely our luck would turn, too.

Indeed, Amphi High School declared a Rachel Brennan Day in May 1997. Emblazoned across the giant marquee in front of the school Rachel's name greeted us as we drove through the entrance for her day of tribute. We met with Mr. Gomez, who'd arranged this honor, and various other teachers, some of whom Rachel knew from the old days. My eyes filled with tears as people recounted "Rachel" stories, her campaign for student body vice president led by the sprint girls on the track team, who'd devised her jingle: *Vote for Brennan / cause she be winnin'*. Outside the cafeteria, we admired her name on several gold plaques, one of which was for state champion of Arizona, another for most valuable player, and the most impressive, received at her graduation, for the school's most valuable female athlete.

In the evening, at the convocation for honors students held in the huge high school assembly, Rachel was presented with yet another plaque. Before her name was called, the superintendent of schools delivered a short speech, and Rachel, from her place in the audience, shouted *RIGHT ON* too loudly, eliciting a titter from the crowd—a small foreshadowing of what would come when, on the stage accepting her honor, she seized the microphone and proceeded to make a few inappropriate wisecracks, beginning, as usual, with the first few lines of the Gettysburg Address, which elicited more titters, but these were uneasy titters. I felt myself blushing furiously.

WHEN WE LEFT Salt Lake, I had the fanciful notion that we'd never return. I'd packed up our household after all, and Tucson was where Rachel once belonged. But the fact was that I had no real job in Tucson. (In academics, the "real" job—tenure-track or tenured—is distinguished always from the less-secure instructorships, which are generally contract positions, thus unreliable as long-term careers.) In addition, we were running out of money; my precious NEA had trickled away. We really had no choice but to return.

Before we did, however, we took another trip, this time

back to San Miguel de Allende with John, who had never been there. Of all the places in the world, San Miguel is the place I'd most want to live. I'm here now, writing this book, looking at the glorious bougainvillea outside the window of my colonial apartment. In the summer of 1997, it had been two years since I'd been in San Miguel, two years since I received the phone call about Rachel's accident. Though we'd hauled the wheelchair with us, Rachel mainly used her walker during our two-week vacation in San Miguel. The walker was a disaster. Rachel could not negotiate the cobbled streets or narrow stone sidewalks; we took taxis everywhere, even from one side of the street to the other.

But the wonderful, almost blessed thing that occurred in 1997 in San Miguel, where our Guadalupe always prevails, is that Rachel began to paint. I enrolled her in an art class where she'd spend four hours a day working on large self-portraits and smaller collages. Her gifted teacher, Carolyn King, who has a disabled daughter of her own, knew instinctively what Rachel needed and how to work around her frustrations. Every day we'd pick up Rachel in a taxi, and she would greet us in good spirits, happy about her artwork. *No restlessness!!!*

As if to spur us into the courage we needed for our trek back to a future of snow and hills, the Guadalupe again manifested herself: this time in the form of a newspaper article about an image of her that had appeared on the surface of a sawed-off tree limb in—guess where?—Salt Lake City, Utah. So we had our sign. We were going home.

It was August and it was hot hot hot. Our Second Avenue

house already looked abandoned, even though I hadn't half-finished packing. Right before we left, Steve presented Rachel with another magnificent present: an Amigo, a motorized handicapped vehicle similar to, but safer than, a golf cart. Rachel's Amigo was the *Baha* model, a kind of all-terrain vehicle equipped with hard rubber tires for rolling over rough roads and an easy, ultrasensitive steering wheel requiring only one hand. Margot and I stood on the Second Avenue porch and watched her speed down the street in her new "car." In spite of ourselves and, in spite of Rachel's erratic maneuvers, Margot and I began to laugh. We clutched each other as Rachel veered dangerously toward the curb, turned a corner, and disappeared from view. We couldn't stop laughing. Who knew where she was headed? She was on her way.

12

WE RETURNED TO Salt Lake in August 1997. John drove us in my new Camry—I'd traded in the Nissan at a Tucson Budget Rent-a-Car sale—and our household would soon follow in a moving van.

Our first stop in Salt Lake was the Guadalupe "shrine" on the corner of Seventh East and Third South, a soulless intersection flanked by social service agency buildings and a highly graffiti-ed city bus shelter: an unlikely place for an apparition. By late summer, spring's sighting in the tree-trunk grain had been lovingly decorated with colorful, slightly grimy plastic flowers, rows of squat, lit votive candles, a donation coffee can with a slot, a padded kneeler on a church pew frame, and a rickety ladder leading to the sawed-off limb which, it seemed to me even from the ground, clearly held the image of Guadalupe surrounded by her mantle of stars.

We made our way up the precarious ladder, John and I possibly more cautiously than Rachel, who is intrepid on stairs of any sort. The trunk of the tree was papered with ornate greeting cards and messages scrawled on scraps of paper, like a bulletin board, and, here and there, a dried bouquet of roses or a corsage from someone's prom. Close-up, the image of the Virgin looked as if it might have been created with a wood-burning tool, but I suspended my disbelief and cried anyway. I was genuinely moved; as the tears ran down my face, I was filled with—oh, how to describe these lofty sentiments unsentimentally except to say that suddenly, for a moment, all my skepticism vanished. It was as if all the suffering of the past two years hadn't occurred, and I was returned wholly to the place of myself, hopeful, optimistic, open to discoveries.

A glance in his direction told me that John was moved, too. His eyes were moist. As for Rachel, she had situated herself on the kneeler in front of the image of Guadalupe, not weeping, but with her eyes tightly closed, her face solemn and radiant. *She* was said to be weeping too: an oily substance oozed from the tree's grain, and we used it to bless ourselves before we climbed down.

But, really, no matter how the image of Guadalupe arrived on the sawed-off limb of the tree on Seventh East and Third South in Salt Lake City, whether the divine had had some human assistance or not, we were all impressed by the shrine. Rachel waxed particularly enthusiastic. "That was so, so wonderful," she said, over and over. For me, any brush with Guadalupe brought a feeling of strength and peace—made me feel as if I could do the impossible without losing my mind. Especially now, in the throes of relocation, with—at best—a difficult year ahead, I felt heartened by Guadalupe's welcome. "There are no wrong moves," a friend once advised me in regard to writing a novel, and I thought of this now as we drove the Camry down First Avenue toward the condo we'd soon make our home.

Nineteen ninety-seven was the first year that the Bulls met the Jazz in the playoffs. Some of the games took place in Salt Lake, and I'd visited in May, both to see a game with Margot and to find Rachel and myself a place to live. The condo, situated close to downtown Salt Lake, in a '70s-type building, was equipped with narrow, iron-railed balconies, beige wall-to-wall carpeting, and a kitchen with an electric stove. Of the above, I liked only the balcony, which afforded, on a good day, a view of the Great Salt Lake floating beyond the city's few skyscrapers: a shimmery swath of silver over which the sun set dramatically.

In fact, the practical perks of the condo substantially outweighed the aesthetic. There was an elevator; there was covered parking in a large cement garage; there was a garage entrance to the lobby with the fake oak paneling that surrounded the manager's Plexiglas window. With minimal difficulty, Rachel could scoot her Amigo into the elevator, go out through the lobby and garage, up First Avenue toward her favorite coffee shop, Java Joe's, or downtown, with me alongside, for a movie or mall trip.

I began my classes with that special zeal that fills only those who have taken a year off. Plus, teaching felt like a

time-out from Rachel duty—a completely guilt-free preoc-
cupation. I was giving a course on contemporary American
literature, and I chose the unlikely (for me) theme of morality and ethics. My course theme reflected my personal life.
Now that the need for action had been thrust upon me, and
I'd allowed myself to be dragged into activity like a zoned-
out, baffled character from Camus, my challenge was to do
the right thing.

But the aftershocks of Rachel's accident were so over-
whelming and complicated that the path to right action wasn't
always clear. Should I, for example, allow Rachel to fritter
away money without consequences? Should I buy her anything she wanted at the mall? Should she be able to drink
mochas all day long? Well, *no*. On the other hand, if buying
Gap T-shirts and drinking flavored lattés made her happy,
who was I to stomp on her few pleasures?

This was my moral dilemma, so to speak. I had raised four
children in a permissive environment. Their good natures
had allowed me my freedom, as it had allowed them theirs. I
was the fun mom, the mom you could talk to, not the mom
who reminded you to make your bed or grounded you for
violating a curfew. Now I was called upon to actually discipline someone. And I tried my best to discipline Rachel, but
her short-term memory was too daunting a problem. She'd
forget our conversations; her sweet agreeableness at the
moment of a serious talk would fade after five minutes. I didn't
have the heart (or the temperament) to be a drill sergeant.

Thus, in the face of her resistance to therapy and any kind
of day program, I made no particular plans for Rachel. I took
the path of least resistance. She was, by now, capable of being
left on her own for hours at a time, though the Amigo, to be

sure, would add to my worries down the line. Every morning, Rachel—always more a creature of routine than her
mother—would fix her own bowl of cereal, climb on her
Amigo, and head off to Java Joe's for her mocha. I, on the
other hand, would prop myself up in bed with a syllabus or a
lesson plan or a piece of student writing or, depending on the
day, would drive to school to teach or meet with students
individually. Always, at the back of my mind, if not in the
forefront, loomed my worries about Rachel: whether she was
driving the Amigo safely on the busy Salt Lake streets,
whether she'd use good judgment with the assorted people
she encountered and inevitably befriended, whether she'd
remember where we lived and not betake herself to the third
floor of a neighboring apartment complex, as she once did,
only to come upon an unfamiliar woman (*not Mom at all!*) at
the door of the apartment she thought was ours.

Rachel continued to have the atypical brain injury profile—girl-on-the-go, restless to the extreme. While the meds
kept her steadier, I cannot say she was especially happy. The
Zoloft and Depakote had quelled the tantrums and severe
depression, but she was still fidgety and bored. She had, as
she put it, "no life." And, of course, what life she had she
couldn't remember.

The restlessness seemed more neurological than psychological to me, although it may have been a bit of both. This
was the year when many books on ADHD (attention deficit
hyperactivity disorder) hit the Barnes & Noble shelves, and I
remember flipping through at least ten books and taking
those little quizzes on Rachel's behalf. I decided that Rachel
must be hyperactive and that if only she were prescribed
some Ritalin, she would settle down. I believed—possibly

because of the success of her current medications—that somewhere a chemical remedy existed for her compulsion to be on the move. Ultimately, Dr. Wagner would advise that we hold off on the Ritalin, reminding me of Rachel's overblown reaction to Dexedrine when she was still hospitalized. This made sense to me, so I gritted my teeth and made a greater effort to tolerate Rachel's restlessness.

Now that I was back at my full-time job, involving not only classes and students but also faculty and committee meetings and extracurricular professional obligations, I felt acutely torn between my career and keeping Rachel safely occupied. It would go like this. I'd arrive home after a day of teaching, and there would be Rachel, disconsolate, having forgotten, despite reminder notes, where I was or when I'd be returning. Rachel: "Where were you, Girlfriend?" Me: "At school. I teach today." Rachel: "So what are we going to do now?" Me: "I need to relax, sit down for a while." Rachel: "I haven't done a thing all day. I'm so bored. This is no life." Me: "But I'm too tired to go out right now, Rache. I've worked all day, and also I have to read this stuff for tomorrow." Rachel: "I hate my life. I'm so bored. I CAN'T STAND THIS! WHAT AM I SUPPOSED TO DO?"

Usually, she'd win, and we'd go off to the mall and buy something or eat something, me anxiously consulting my watch, assessing whether I had enough time to read and prepare for the next day's classes. Once at home: "How about we go out for some ice cream? I did nothing all day long!!"

So our lives would go, an uneasy compromise between Rachel's requirements and the requirements of my job. Truthfully, I felt as though I were failing at both. Rachel cruised the streets of Salt Lake and I tore my nails off between classes, worrying about her. Meanwhile, word had spread in the English Department that I was a woman with her share of troubles, that I could not quite be counted on. In the fall graduate student writing contest, I was not asked to read any work. When I confronted a colleague about this "oversight," she told me that she was trying to protect me. "Please don't," I said. I felt strongly that I needed to re-assert myself as a full-fledged member of the English Department, but even the students were wary and kept their distance. Having resigned as director of the Creative Writing Program, I found myself in the unhappy role that burned-out professors slip into once they have lost their usefulness and spark: deadweight.

Moreover, after a year's absence, my friends were no longer as available as they had been in our moments of crisis. Who could blame them? We'd been away, for one thing, and for another, I knew that my life with Rachel presented certain social difficulties. One colleague put it to me bluntly: "People don't invite you because they know you have to bring Rachel." It was true: When I wasn't working, Rachel and I were joined at the hip. She accompanied me to faculty get-togethers, to the infrequent movie date with a friend, and, at times, to school, where she'd roam the corridors making embarrassing and inappropriate quips to all who passed by. I spent a lot of time wincing. I spent a lot of time apologizing, then realizing the wrongheadedness of my apologies.

As for Rachel, her secret life was in full swing. She went god-knows-where during the days I taught and did god-knows-what. Not a shred of memory remained after her day was done. Once a middle-aged, neatly dressed Hispanic man came to our door and asked for *Raquel*. Rachel came to the door and greeted him like an old friend. She patted him on the back. "Que tal, amigo?" When he left, I asked her how she knew him. "I have no idea," she confessed with a giggle.

"You can't tell people where we live," I told her. "It's dangerous."

"He's a perfectly nice guy, Girlfriend. I think I must have met him at the mall."

So we had another talk. And another talk. If repetition was her pathology, it was becoming my disciplinary rod. Sooner or later, I felt something would sink in. (Though it's odd, come to think of it, that we use such expressions—"sink in" and "stick"—as if the brain were a trap and life were the wild animal evading it.)

One afternoon I arrived home to find her bruised and scraped—obvious road rash. "I'm not sure what happened," she said. "Maybe I fell off my Amigo. Maybe someone helped me up. But I really have no idea how this happened."

Then there were the phone calls from strangers, usually beginning with "I have a young woman here who says she's lost." Then off I'd go in the Camry to some odd address, miles away. "I must have gotten confused," she'd say. And since I couldn't lift the extremely heavy Amigo and put it in the car, I'd drive slowly alongside Rachel and her vehicle until we reached the condo building on First Avenue. Of course, riding alongside didn't work when the Amigo's battery was dead; then we'd call a cab and hope that the driver's muscles were up to the task.

This happened in the middle of downtown once, just at dusk. I'd given Rachel a cell phone, and she called from a location she couldn't describe and told me the Amigo's battery was dead.

"What's the name of the street?" I kept pleading with her. "Look up at the corner for a street sign."

"I just can't see one, Girlfriend," she said.

"WELL ASK SOMEONE WHERE YOU ARE! JUST STOP SOMEONE AND ASK! YOU'RE GOOD AT THAT!" It was getting dark, and I was frantic and shouting into the phone.

Finally, she managed to convey a garbled location—something about a Burger King next to a gray brick building—and I literally ran downtown, where, after an hour of searching, I discovered her (and the Amigo, which was half off the curb) chatting with a group of skateboarders, her backward baseball cap matching theirs. A taxi took us home that night, but what she'd been doing in the heart of downtown Salt Lake, where she'd been headed, we'd never know.

In an attempt to provide some kind of daytime activity for Rachel, I arranged for her to attend a YWCA volunteer orientation meeting. The women's Y in Salt Lake is renowned for its women's shelter, which, at the time, was directed by our good friend Shelley. Rachel was insulted by the whole idea of volunteerism—she felt she should be able to have a salaried job. We went over and over it—*being a volunteer is a step toward a regular job, who knows—the Y might hire you after a few months of volunteering, just think of the contribution you could make with your Spanish proficiency* (Salt Lake has a thriving Hispanic community), and so on.

I had high hopes for the Y. Rachel's people skills, aside from her inappropriateness, were mainly good: She was friendly, warm, compassionate. Moreover, the Y's atmosphere was casual; it had an almost alternative feeling. Women in jeans with pierced noses and eyebrows, their hair dyed spectacular

shades of platinum and purple, rushed around the old building, arms full of files, obviously committed to their cause and
jobs. I thought Rachel's social mishaps might be tolerated here.

At the orientation meeting, which was attended by twelve
wannabe volunteers, I tried to remain inconspicuous. I
wanted Rachel to be in charge of herself. I sat at one end of
the long table, and Rachel sat close to the coordinator of volunteers, a middle-aged woman named Tracey, at the other.
Tracey started off with roundtable introductions. When it
was Rachel's turn, I held my breath. I could see the corners of
her mouth working mischievously. "I was born a small black
child," she began, quoting that famous line from the Steve
Martin movie, *The Jerk*. She got a laugh, but it was an uneasy
laugh. I stared at my lap.

Tracey was well-meaning, but tedious in her presenta-
tion. Once or twice I glanced at Rachel, who had begun to
fidget. I could tell she was dying to interrupt and change the
mood. I was fidgety myself. Tracey was giving the volunteer
and resident rule book a thorough going-over. The other
would-be volunteers were busily taking notes in the folder
provided to them. At one point, Rachel yawned loudly and I
gave her a look. "Excuse me," she said, giggling.

When Tracey got to the rules for smoking—*not in the
house, but on the patio, and only at certain times, and once again,
never in the rooms, but there is the patio, over there,* et cetera—
Rachel could no longer restrain herself. She raised her hand,
and I could tell from the tongue-in-cheek expression on her
face that whatever was coming, it wouldn't be what Tracey
wanted to hear. I signaled madly from my end of the table.
NO, I mouthed to Rachel, who caught my eye, *DON'T.* But
Tracey, as luck would have it, called on Rachel. "I was just

wondering," said Rachel, pausing for dramatic and comic effect, "are the women allowed to bring their CRACK PIPES to this facility?" A nervous titter went around the table. I caught the eye of someone, a young woman wearing a wool poncho, who looked as if she might be sympathetic. "Just wondering," said Rachel, shrugging her shoulders. "Just asking."

Nevertheless, Rachel managed a short volunteer stint at the Y. She organized someone's office, she entered data in a ledger. She hated it. And, after a while, she was not asked back. I was never quite sure if her behavior was the cause or if the Y genuinely didn't need someone with Rachel's level of skill, but, after three or four times, we were told she was not needed.

To reintegrate us both into a social community of some sort, I decided to entertain. I hardly had the time to do this, but I was lonely and missed having friends around us. Rachel loved nothing better than a social gathering. We'd been spoiled by Jane and Kim and company in Tucson. Moreover, Srinivas and Ranjii, my mainstays in the pre-Tucson days, had taken jobs in Seattle, and my old friend Tom was shuttling back and forth to Minnesota to be with his wife, Disa. I felt extremely bereft. Plus, I liked to give parties. I liked planning and arranging flowers and sprucing up the house, and I liked cooking.

My first party was a shower for Tom and Disa, who were expecting a baby. Disa flew in from Minnesota, and I invited almost the entire faculty and, among other things, served homemade pizzas and M. F. K. Fisher's gingersnaps. (Let this be my nod to the mention of chic food so trendy among writers of memoir.) I cranked up Billie Holiday on the stereo and attended to the pizzas (I wouldn't recommend these for a big party—too labor intensive) while Rachel worked the crowd. From time to time, I checked on her where she sat cuddling a baby or recounting the story of her accident to a glazed-eyed audience.

Still, our guests seemed to enjoy themselves, and Tom and Disa received loads of great gifts for their baby-to-be. After everyone left, Rachel whipped the kitchen into shape, joyous in the aftermath of attention and laughter. Before bed, we cranked up Marvin Gaye and danced in our sparkling kitchen, me supporting my big daughter in my arms as we swayed in our best Motown groove. The pre-accident Rachel had been a terrific dancer, gifted with both athletic grace and natural rhythm. Since the accident, her sense of rhythm was impaired: It was all she could do to tap a painfully skewed beat with her good left hand. She was hearing it, I believed, but couldn't quite reproduce it.

But here she was in my arms and she felt wonderful, my girl, even as I dragged her, laughing, from counter to counter. In moments like these, I realized how blessed I was to be with Rachel, to have that much love in my life, and, corny as it may sound, to have the privilege of being her caregiver and mother.

WINTER PRESENTED A particular challenge that year. In the mornings, I'd hear the big snowplows crunch down First Avenue, and I'd know we were in for it, Rachel and me. Me, because I'd have trouble driving to school—one morning, what is normally a five-minute drive, at most, took me an hour in bumper-to-bumper traffic, cars tailspinning off the road or being pushed out of snowbanks by helpful passersby.

And Rachel, because she'd be homebound that day, which tested her endurance to the limit. After such days, I'd arrive home to her inevitable tears of frustration, as if the snowstorm had been created especially to torment her.

In late November, we attended the Brain Injury Conference in Park City. The keynote speaker was a Holocaust survivor, an energetic seventy-something woman. "Close your eyes," she instructed the audience. "Try to imagine that everything in your life as you know it has disappeared. Whoever you were in the past is dead. Your relationships, your abilities, your very unique way of encountering the world have altered radically. You are a person you no longer recognize and so you keep yearning for an old self that will never return."

No, I thought, this cannot be imagined. For two plus years, I'd been trying to imagine what it was like inside Rachel's head, and I'd been unable to summon up anything that made sense. I opened my eyes and looked around the room. There was Frances, Eric's wife, her eyes tightly shut. Only twenty-one, Eric had been severely injured in a car accident one year ago. He sat beside her in his wheelchair, a long string of drool sliding from the side of his mouth. I couldn't tell if Eric's eyes were closed, but surely he had no need to imagine any of this.

Rachel had long since Amigo-ed from the room in search of more interesting pastimes. "This is amazingly boring," she'd announced before, too loudly, and with contempt. Others were dutiful; like Frances, they kept their eyes closed and their lips set, trying to imagine. Next to me, one of the survivors—the brain injured are called *survivors* these days—fiddled with a zipper on his jacket, scratched his head.

Instead, with my eyes wide open, without any effort at all, I was remembering a girl competing in a PAC 10 race in Phoenix, then the same girl trying flowered underpants on her head, a long piece of blond grass dangling from her mouth. This girl has freckles, and when she laughs I see some gaps in her smile, missing teeth; flash forward, and I'm hugging her again at the airport, the last time I hugged the old Rachel. She feels so little in my arms, even at twenty-four.

Unlike Rachel, I have no trouble making narratives. In 1995, I hugged her at an airport curbside, and the next time I saw her she was a different person. Hence my story is one of loss, and I construct myself that way: I am the grieving mother, exhausted, long-suffering, no longer quite so vivacious, clinging reasonably or unreasonably (depending on the day) to my faith in my daughter's recovery. My "identity," though not enviable at this juncture, has at least the virtue of situating me here, in this life which is mine.

A bit later, I scoured the corridors of the Yarrow, thankfully not a large hotel, looking for Rachel. I even poked my head in the kitchen, since Rachel is apt to seek out Spanish speakers and she knows where, in our Utah culture, to find them. After forty-five minutes, I began to panic. I asked the bearded guy at the EEG booth to keep an eye out, also a brain injury conference monitor by the name of Lois, and Tammy, the front-desk clerk who had a pierced tongue. Everyone's brows furrowed in consternation.

Then I heard her. "Girlfriend Jones?" she called out to me. She was holding a latté and waving with the latté hand, splashing on her white shirt. "Over here!" she shouted. "Girlfriend Smith," I shouted back. "Thank God."

Then, in mid-January, my father tripped over a shoe in my parents' Florida condo and broke his hip. "This is the last lap. I'm on my way out," he told me long-distance, from his hospital bed, characteristically irreverent. I could picture his wry grin. Though I never would have believed it at the time, these would be the last words he would speak to me. I made three cross-country trips to Florida during February and March, missing weeks of classes, frantically arranging for Rachel-care, until that March morning when my sister and brothers and I agreed to disconnect our father's life supports and, surrounding his bed, held him until he died, forty-five minutes later.

Rachel flew in for the funeral with Geoff, her second Florida visit since the accident. On the first, when we'd flown in from Tucson for my mother's eightieth birthday, my father, who'd not been an especially patient person, had been amazingly patient and understanding with Rachel. "Hey apple-head! Hey chowderhead!" he'd call to her in the mornings, which delighted her. I have a photograph of the two of them, grandfather and granddaughter, arms around each other at the celebration dinner, my dad looking more fragile than I ever remember him being, and Rachel looking healthier and more alert than we gave her credit for in those days.

So, in a bizarre turn that only real life can provide, and despite my profound grief, my father's death proved to be the beginning of our trek back to productivity and luck. That spring quarter I wrote my first non-Rachel piece of fiction since the accident—a story based on my father's death called "The Soul in Its Flight." And I was teaching one of those graduate fiction workshops that comes along once a lifetime—a class that clicks.

I organized the course around readings that, in creative-writing-speak, "transgress genre boundaries." That is to say, fiction which leaks into nonfiction and even poetry. I must have been tending toward such leakages (a Rachel word) in my own work, or rather in the subconscious of my future work, having begun to realize, I suppose, the inviolability of the actual life, its absolute, undeniable presence in imaginative writing. Also, wasn't I living a life whose boundaries had been dismantled? My sense of the world had radically altered, along with Rachel's, and I felt called upon to express this new state of affairs, its messy parameters.

For Rachel, spring brought freedom from the condo-jail, and so she was able to speed off to Java Joe's each morning, making her way through the blaze of Salt Lake's flower-lined streets, the rows of chestnuts, maple, and oak. We had begun physical therapy again, at Deb Wagner's suggestion, and Rachel was now walking quite well with a four-pronged cane. We decorated the cane with glued-on sparkles and stars, and on the four-prong's bottom platform I created a silly scene out of tiny plastic dinosaurs and he-men and fake grass. Around this time, someone gave Rachel a bumper sticker for her Amigo: *Girls Kick Ass*. While we loved this, it seemed to alarm some of the condo residents, who were elderly and devout.

At the advice of Deb Wagner, I signed Rachel up for vocational rehabilitation. I should mention that I have a horror of these state programs. In Tucson, I'd spent hours in a pea-green waiting room with a restless, close to raving Rachel trying to initiate her social security insurance. Though it came through in Tucson, it had been nearly impossible in Utah. No one in the Salt Lake Social Security office ever answered the phone, and, then, on one occasion we waited almost three hours in a similar waiting room only to be handed an array of forms that took months to process.

Voc rehab, I was sure, would produce mountains of red tape. But we made an appointment at the Seventh South office anyway, stopping briefly beforehand to visit the Guadalupe shrine. *Help us, please,* I asked the Virgin, who was still weeping oil, which I put to our tongues.

Our caseworker sat in a darkened office surrounded by mostly empty bookshelves. Mr. Waverly. Reaching into a file drawer, he removed a thick packet of forms, set them on the table in front of him, and unscrewed the top of his fountain pen.

"What do you want to do, Rachel?"

"Well," said Rachel, sounding very reasonable and confident, "I'd like to go to medical school."

"No, no, Rache," I said, rolling my eyes at Mr. Waverly. "You can't go to medical school at this point."

"Maybe some day," said Mr. Waverly, smiling faintly.

Then I explained about Rachel's short-term memory problem, her injury and so forth. Mr. Waverly sighed and fetched more forms.

"I don't see why I can't go to medical school," Rachel insisted a few more times.

So went our first voc rehab visit. There would be more. Eventually, it was decided that voc rehab would try to find her a job as a teaching assistant in a school bilingual program. If med school was out, at least she wanted to find a way to use her Spanish.

A job coach met us in Mr. Waverly's office one afternoon. A mild-mannered man wearing a yellow windbreaker, Bill laughed pleasantly at Rachel's wisecracks and seemed to think she was employable. What a job coach does is to accompany the employee to the job until the employee is oriented to the employment tasks. In Rachel's case, the job coach would be especially vital. Finding her way to classrooms and learning names and procedures would be a tremendous challenge for her. But, of course, she resented the concept of a job coach. After all, she genuinely believed she was ready for medical school.

So it was that Rachel went to her first job interview accompanied by Bill. We found an outfit at Nordstrom—a red-knit sweater with pull-on elastic-waisted pants to match. Her power suit, we joked. She rode Flex-tran that day, the disability bus, and Bill brought her home. "How did it go?" I asked Rachel when she returned. "Great," she said.

That evening, Bill telephoned with another story. Apparently, the interview *had* gone smoothly, for the most part— Rachel answered questions intelligently, she demonstrated her Spanish skills adequately, she was almost a shoo-in. Then the team of interviewers asked Rachel if she had any questions for them. Rachel had looked around at the three or four interviewers and settled on the principal, who—I discovered this later from the girl with "no memory"—had a weird haircut. ("Bi-level," Rachel reported, "with little bangs.") So this was her question: "Yeah, where do you get your hair done?"

"That just about did it," said Bill sadly.

"I see," I said, engulfed by disappointment.

So, for a long while, this was the end of voc rehab for Rachel.

My father had left me some money in his will, and I realized that I could actually afford to buy a house. House hunting, however, was a daunting prospect. I simply didn't have the time. Then my good friend and colleague, poet Mark Doty, made me an offer I couldn't refuse. I'd known Mark for years and was instrumental in his hire, but, as life's circumstances would have it, his first year at the University of Utah had coincided with our year off in Tucson, and we hadn't seen each other much. Now that we'd re-ignited our friendship and I'd become close friends with his partner, fiction writer Paul Lisicky, as well, Mark had decided to accept a position at the University of Houston. Just my luck, I thought sadly. Mark must have read my disappointed mind. "Buy my house. The writing vibes are great," he said, referring to his beautifully restored Victorian on Third Avenue. "I want you and Rachel to have it and I'll give you a great deal." Which he did.

So Mark and Paul were gone—I was ticking off my best friends, year by year—but in their place we had the house of my dreams.

13

I am crying like a small but detailed tree.
— Rachel's journal, 1999

WE MOVED INTO our new home in June, our fourth move in two years. But it was worth it. After the boxes were unpacked and broken down, after the cupboards and closets were filled with our dishes and clothes, after the pictures were hung, the furniture arranged, the refrigerator stocked, we settled down in the moss green living room with its vintage gas fireplace and counted our blessings.

That was the summer I harvested the apricots from the huge backyard tree and made jam. I used a ladder and a broom to knock bunches of cherries off of another taller, skinnier tree (before the worms got to them) and made cobblers. I even found a few raspberries in a clump of soft leaves and popped them in our mouths.

The house, built in 1896, worked on my imagination. In the kitchen, stirring my big pot of preserves, I could almost see myself as a turn-of-the-century woman, polishing the woodwork, crocheting afghans, though I never did either of these things. Instead, I bought an array of wines from our local wine store and invited friends over. This would be our new beginning, I could feel it. (Though even as I told myself these words, I recalled the irony of a Ray Carver character who proclaimed, at the story's dark ending, "My life is going to change. I can feel it." And you, the reader, know it doesn't have a prayer of changing.)

At any rate, we had everything we needed. Rachel's bedroom was big enough to hold her double bed and her stationary bike; mine was even bigger, with long windows overlooking a row of lovely turn-of-the-century houses across the street. Two baths, one up, one down—though I would soon long for my own upstairs bathroom, the Rachel ablutions being too time-consuming to compete with. But then I had a study, very small, with just enough room for bookcases and a desk. It was in this room that Mark had completed at least one volume of poetry, that he had written his new memoir, *Firebird*. The writing vibes would be good.

Best of all, from a financial perspective, the house had a charming garden-level rental which paid half the mortgage. I think my wheeler-dealer dad, from beyond the grave, had something to do with that part. Unmistakably a bargain.

But just as everything seemed close to blissful, the Rachel troubles started up again. Suddenly, her meds were not keeping her steady. The screaming commenced and persisted. Moreover, she fell somehow and hurt her knee, which made riding the stationary bike painful and, eventually, impossible. At a dinner full of friends one night, she had a violent outburst of rage and tears, stunning everyone.

I must have made eight trips to the emergency room that summer, where we'd wait for hours to see a resident. "There's nothing wrong with her knee," pronounced a resident, after a cursory examination. "Perhaps a tranquilizer," suggested another. At home, Rachel's knee pain was so severe her entire leg would seize up in spasms. Eventually, we were able to see a sports medicine doctor who arranged for an MRI. The image, due to Rachel's fidgeting in the chamber, was fuzzy and practically unreadable, but it showed a tear of the anterior cruciate ligament (ACL), the classic basketball injury. The doctor, bright-eyed, handsome, young, almost alarmingly upbeat, suggested that the ACL might be an old injury—acquired during her athletic years.

"But wouldn't she have known if she'd torn her ACL in the past?" I asked the doctor.

"Not necessarily," he said cheerfully.

So we had no clear diagnosis, and Rachel's knee pain did not subside for months. This meant the stationary bike was off-limits, and Rachel's mood swings grew worse. Even I had underestimated the value of the endorphin rushes that followed her workouts. And in a neighborhood where, especially in the summers, kids and their moms traveled the sidewalks in front of our house, pushing bicycles and drawing big hopscotch squares with pastel chalk, Rachel's screams rang loud and scary. It occurred to me that our neighbors might think I was torturing her.

One Sunday afternoon, following an especially intense outburst, during which she and I both screamed, she at life, me at her to shut up, I stood on my front porch and took several deep breaths. I caught my neighbor's eye as he wheelbarrowed a heap of weeds to his compost. A burly, kind man who has since become our friend, he looked at me with a mixture of compassion and bewilderment, and I felt I had to say something.

"Look, Rachel is going through a very hard time now. I'm not abusing her." I'd attempted an ironic tone, but our neighbor simply nodded. He might have been holding a rake. Seconds later, tears rolled down my cheeks. I was thinking: Does he believe me? Does he wish we'd never moved in, this peculiar mother and daughter? Or does he just feel sorry for us? Any of the above would have been humiliating. And when I returned to the house, shutting the old oak door with its brass bell behind me, I felt like I'd entered the mad and impermeable world of that peculiar mother and daughter, the crazy and the crazier, and I had a vision of us growing old there, bedridden, worn out by a lifetime of coping.

During all this, my children from their far and wide locales kept in constant touch with us. Margot and Geoff played bad and good cop with Rachel, Margot giving the "shape-up" speech, the butt-kicking don't-feel-so-sorry-for-yourself-you-have-a-lot-to-be-thankful-for motivational talk that Rachel probably needed and welcomed on some level, while patient Geoff spent long hours listening to Rachel's rants, talking her down. I depended on Geoff especially, who, any time of day or night, was available to talk to us. Chris, who, due to his own life circumstances, was less available than Margot or Geoff, was always gentle and somewhat careful with Rachel on the telephone, and I could hear the sadness in his voice when we spoke, as if it had been up to him to prevent all this trouble from befalling our family.

Geoff invited Rachel to San Francisco for a long weekend in July: "To give you a break, Mom," he said. Rachel boarded the plane on a Friday, met several travelers on the flight who, according to Geoff, accompanied her out the gate, merrily exchanging addresses and phone numbers. Rachel's mood swings made her euphoric half the time, and the euphoria was catching. People loved to be around her when she was in this mood—she was funny, observant, and altogether charming, especially to strangers.

Geoff's experience that weekend wasn't so upbeat. He called every few hours, reporting the latest crisis. Rachel punched him on the arm while he was driving; refused to go to a park if she had to ride in a wheelchair; screamed at him when he was taking naps. "And she's always complaining," he said. "Shit, Mom, I don't know how you can take it." She was, he declared at the end of her visit, "a nightmare." Among them, my children decided I was spoiling Rachel, allowing her to get away with too much, waiting on her too much. I received a few well-meaning lectures, which, in fact, I agreed with, even though I couldn't seem to find an alternative behavior.

In late summer, Dr. Wagner returned from vacationing with her family, and she listened seriously as I described the latest Rachel woes. Even so, she was able to pronounce Rachel much better than before, more alert, more cognizant in every way. Eventually, we decided to change the medications—deep-six the Zoloft and try Prozac. I knew from my Internet wanderings that Zoloft had a reputation for becoming ineffectual after a year, and it had been at least a year. Of course, stopping Zoloft took at least two weeks, and beginning Prozac would take another two. That would be a full month before any changes in mood. I resigned myself to it.

In the interim, I looked into rehab places for Rachel. It occurred to me that there might be some place, somewhere, that took people like Rachel and got them back on their feet, so to speak. Certainly, my attempts at structuring her days had failed miserably, and we couldn't go on like this, could we? I found a place, ultimately, that seemed perfect—a facility in California called Ray of Hope, which catered to the brain injured and to stroke victims, providing apartments with supervision, therapies, recreational groups, and vocational guidance. The goal was, in rehab-speak, *re-entry*. It sounded good to me. There were a couple of catches. The first catch was that Ray of Hope was in another state and might not be covered by Rachel's Utah Medicaid. If it wasn't, it would be prohibitively expensive. The other catch was that there was not a slot available for Rachel.

Rachel was so volatile at this point, there was no containing her. I rented out our garden-level apartment to two young and resourceful women, and they would report to me on the screams I didn't hear when I was at school. I practiced endurance, taking naps, busying myself with work. I was writing stories again and teaching a class which challenged me called "The Emergence of Modernism." To distract myself, I wrote a story called "The Emergence of Modernism," a pastiche of memoir, criticism, and modernist allusion. I was beginning to realize that only in the throes of writing could I remove myself from the pain at hand. Perhaps, this is always the case for writers: Writing provides a way to steer the mind elsewhere. Then, gradually, the Prozac took hold and we were free again. Rachel calmed down; she returned to her cheerful self. And I to mine.

THOUGH WHAT IS A "self," if not a complex of chemicals, I wondered? What is a "self" at all? How odd that wit and intelligence and even sensitivity could be doused in a heart-beat, only to leave—what?—dullness and rage in their places. "Who's there?" is the opening line of *Hamlet*, which is nothing if not a play about the slippery issue of identity. Who's there, indeed? I mused as I watched Rachel clomp up the porch steps, as I gazed at my own face in the mirror.

Rachel's identity is, it seems to me, both the same and not the same, her linguistic turns even richer post-injury—mul-tidimensional, associative, pun-laden—as if along a single unfettered trajectory (some neuronal path untouched by cell death or atrophy) she has learned to compensate for her very movement through space, its own flawed narrative. My friend, the writer David Shields, who visited Utah in the spring of 2000 to give a reading, put it best. After a conversa-tion with Rachel, he said, "I didn't know if I was talking to a three-year-old or to Samuel Beckett."

And though the moods had improved, the knee had not. There was no riding of the stationary bike. Without exercise, Rachel's weight climbed enormously: She was close to two hundred pounds, I was sure of it. Thanks to therapy at the University, she now walked, or lumbered, with a regular cane—one-pronged, not four-pronged—and was so delighted with this achievement that she refused to use the Amigo. The Amigo, in her eyes, had become obsolete, intended only

don't know her situation," said the officer, his
dening to something like disbelief. "She seems
e."

e, there was Rachel, joking with the younger,
dmitting ruefully her encounters with the pizza
g altogether reasonable and even charming.

gment is not good," I explained. "She's recover-
evere brain injury."

I'll need a doctor's notarized note to that effect."
stood up and walked to the door with his blue-
nion.

ant to protect my daughter," I pleaded at the
e, help us out here."

between you and your daughter, ma'am," he said,
ought.

you should have thought of your daughter's morality
go is what he might have been saying. He gave
roving look before swiveling around on my front
marching down the steps to his patrol car.

e's a happy-ish ending to the pizza man story.
came home to find Rachel loudly admonishing
hall. He was trying to kiss her—I saw this—and
her face away. "Don't come back," she told him in
ou're not my friend." And with that, he left.

ad for her judgment and the memory power it
aken to make it, but I was dismayed, am still dis-

Rachel's neediness interferes with her sense of
or it is neediness, I'm convinced, a need to be held
by a man that compels these lapses on Rachel's
he brain injury, per se, but the kind of longing we
ptible to. "Use condoms" is all I now advise.

for those who couldn't walk at all, a terrible symbol of her
disability. And while I respected her need to project a certain
image on the world, not using the Amigo was an inconvenience for both of us. I made the case that the Amigo gave her
independence, that she could motor to the University in ten
short minutes, for example—we now lived a short distance
from the U. But Rachel was adamant.

One Sunday morning, after mass at the cathedral, after
brunch at our favorite Salt Lake restaurant, The Oasis, I per-
suaded her to come up City Creek Canyon with me, using her
Amigo. City Creek, though not far, is a good walk away from
where we live and so, reluctantly, Rachel agreed. No sooner
were we on our way up Memory Grove, the shady old park
that precedes the canyon, than Rachel had one of her melt-
downs. It was a glorious, blue-skied day, and it seemed everyone in Salt Lake had come to the park for recreation. Kids and
adults on fancy mountain bikes, picnickers, lovers, dogs. I had
been feeling exuberant. A flock of joggers passed us in running shorts and Nikes, sweatbands drenched. We could hear
them breathing hard as they angled around us: the girl in the
handicapped cart and her mom, who walked alongside. This
was the reason for the meltdown. "It's too painful," Rachel
sobbed. "It's just too painful to see those runners. Especially
when I remember running up City Creek myself."

I remembered it too. I have a clear picture of Rachel on
the floor of our old Third Avenue house, during one of her
visits from Colorado, pulling on her Nikes and stretching
those beautiful runner's legs. For some reason, I had watched
her legs that pre-accident day: not overly muscled like those
of some athletes but thin-calved, strong-boned, smooth as
silk. Her face held all her pre-run stamina and determina-

tion. I remember saying something to her—who knows what?—and having her look away, intent, disinterested. What I wouldn't give for that cool disinterest today, though, at the time, it wounded me a little.

Tearfully, we made our way home from City Creek. Once or twice Rachel berated me for having the nerve to *walk* at her side. "You're being unreasonable," I said, and I recalled something Dr. Bach had said to me once: "Keep in mind, Karen, that you didn't get on that motorcycle."

"You're being insensitive!" retorted Rachel angrily. When we hit Third Avenue, I climbed on the back of the Amigo to see if this would distract Rachel. But no, she wasn't as stimulus-bound as she used to be. We only looked silly, and the Amigo careened dangerously with my added weight. "Get off," Rachel said, impatiently. So I did. In the evening, I dismantled the Amigo and lugged its batteries and plastic framepieces to the storage room in the basement.

Without the Amigo, Rachel wouldn't be as prone to wandering and getting lost. On the other hand, her travels, confined to our small neighborhood, left her with little to do. In place of Java Joe's, we had, thankfully, a posh cafe and restaurant called Cucina, and this became Rachel's daily hangout. The iced mochas—her beverage of choice—ran about three bucks, at a conservative estimate, and so Cucina was not as cost-effective as it was convenient. Add to that a huge scone, a bowl of fresh fruit, an occasional juice, and we're talking a ten-dollar-a-day habit. That's three hundred bucks a month for Rachel's amusements, not counting the other money I spent on her. But so what? I thought, nervously. It was all she *did*, after all. It was her three-hundred-buck-a-month life.

Well, I suppose it's not
arrived home from schoo
ally that she'd had sex witl
pizza delivery truck.

"You WHAT?"

Rachel was sheepish,
played at the corners of he
fully, to suppress it. I was

"Did you use a condon
"I don't think so, Girlf

He didn't force himsel
clear was the fact that she

"But he never calls," sl
"You mean you *know* t
"Yeah, well, we've don
though, Girlfriend."

I sat on the sofa and
hour. The sinking feeli
remembered (hopefully) t
I drove there and asked
"He's very polite, Hispar
worked the espresso macl
me the name of the piz
Mazda. So I called the co

The Salt Lake police
daughter, warily. "Let me
charge. "Your daughter v
consensual sex with a mar

"I don't want you arro
you to find him at his plac
Rachel's situation."

"But
wariness
all right t

Of co
cuter cop
guy, seem

"Her
ing from

"Ma'a
The offic
eyed com

"I just
door. "Ple

"This
smugly I

*I suppo
a long tim
me a disap
porch and

But th
One day I
him in the
she turned
Spanish. "

I was
must have
mayed, tha
propriety.
and loved
part—not
are all susc

In November, I hired a homeopath to come to the house and treat Rachel. Always on the lookout for miracle cures, I'd heard of this woman from a man who'd been giving Rachel massages and cranio-sacral. The woman, Liz, a large frizzy-haired blond wearing an unlikely floral gown, hefted a giant carpetbag up the steps of our front porch. "Liz," she said, thrusting forth her hand and giving mine a torturous squeeze.

Liz listened in silence to the long list of Rachel's disabilities and pains, then began to fish around in her big bag. At length, she removed four little glass vials of tiny, round, white pills.

"How's the knee pain this very minute?" she asked Rachel. Liz had a brusque way of talking, but I came to love it.

"Bad," Rachel admitted. "It hurts when I walk."

"Stick this under your tongue," Liz instructed Rachel, tipping a tiny pill into Rachel's mouth from its vial.

Liz then consulted her watch for about thirty seconds.

"How's the knee now, Rachel?" she asked.

Rachel smiled. "Amazingly, it doesn't hurt."

"So you notice a difference?" Liz said.

"A difference from what?"

"From the way your knee had been bothering you."

"But my knee doesn't seem to bother me today."

As we were to discover, the bad short-term memory could not be helped with a pill, homeopathic or otherwise. Still, at that moment, Liz was a god to me. I bought several bottles of homeopathic pills, plus a book, *The Materia Medica*, which listed all the homeopathic cures and remedies amassed since the eighteenth century. And I'm convinced that with the aid of whatever it was in that little pill that melted under

Rachel's tongue each morning, the knee continued to improve; soon Rachel was up on her stationary bike, doing double and triple workouts, making up for lost time (though how she sensed this time lost from workouts is another memory mystery).

Shortly after the homeopathic knee miracle, I discovered a back-to-work program offered by the Utah Brain Injury Association. This was a three-month program which actually paid trainees minimum wage to learn office skills and, ultimately, tried to place them in jobs. In order to enroll Rachel, we had to go through voc rehab. The solemn Mr. Waverly had retired, and in his place we were assigned a sprightly, high-strung woman named Penny, whom I liked immediately, despite the fact that she did not inspire confidence. Most of our visit was taken up with an account of Penny's current crises, ranging from the professional to the personal. Well, we'd made a connection, and in the oddball world of disability and social service agencies, that was a rarity. Still, she was having difficulties with her computer, her desk was chaotic, and once or twice she seemed close to tears. My hopes for Rachel were rapidly dwindling. I envisioned months of waiting for the back-to-work program, months of who knew how many more mishaps and phone calls from good samaritans. Nevertheless, Penny assured us that she would get the okay for funds immediately. "No problem," she said, as she riffled through the papers on her desk for the right form, dropped a pencil, and overturned a glass jar of tulips. Incredibly, she came through.

We saw Penny on a Wednesday, and Rachel began at the Brain Injury Association on Monday. She would be gone from nine to three; she would learn some data processing;

she would hang out with other brain injured persons and, hopefully, find some friends. We'd arranged for Flex-tran to transport her both ways. For a while, once again, I was off the hook. I could teach worry-free; and on nonteaching days, I could sit behind my computer and write. Heaven.

The brain injury program lasted about a month and a half, during which Rachel's attendance was slowly cut back. She began by being insulted by the data processing tasks, then graduated to Spanish translation, which made her much more cheerful. "I feel like I'm being of use, finally," she'd report at the end of a Spanish translation day. She had homework with her—the brain injury brochure, which she meticulously translated into perfect Spanish, working hours after work on my computer. But when the brochure translation was completed, it appeared no other translations were in the offing. That left the despised data processing. She complained about it, as well as about her co-workers, the other brain injured, and she was complained about by the neighboring restaurant, where she would stop for coffee or pizza. She was causing a stir there, joking too much with the waitpeople, being overly friendly with the customers. She was bad for business. The brain injury association had been called, and Rachel had been instructed to stay on the premises, which, predictably, she resisted. On one occasion, she tried to walk home—having a clear sense neither of the way nor of the five- or six-mile distance—and was found by some well-meaning person and driven back to the Brain Injury Association. Betty, the program coordinator, had been scouring the neighborhood for her. "We obviously can't have this," Betty told me later.

So, over a period of six weeks, Rachel's time at the back-to-work program was zapped to no time. "Rachel is delightful," Betty assured me. But even Betty's support of Rachel became less enthusiastic as time went on. Rachel was prone to frustration, to willfulness, to tactlessness with the other brain injured trainees. She was inappropriate, she was bratty. I remember visiting on one occasion when Rachel had been assigned telephone duty. When the phone rang, she answered, "Brain-damaged ward." And even though she quickly followed up with a "Just kidding, Girlfriend," and to me, later, "It was only a joke," it seemed we were stuck here in Rachel's world, where the default was set permanently on *joke*. Oh it was funny, oh it was impossible.

Then, a miracle: A caseworker from Ray of Hope, the California rehabilitation center that I'd been badgering for the past six months, came to visit us in our home, to assess Rachel for the program. Rachel unfolded her long-range plans for medical school to the caseworker, who seemed hip to brain injury denial. A grandmotherly type wearing long hoop earrings, she impressed me with her compassion and humor. "She'd be perfect for Ray of Hope," she confided to me at the door. "I'll see what I can do."

So, in February 1998, I flew with Rachel to the California facility, which was situated in a small town near Los Angeles, and enrolled her. She would be living in an apartment complex, kind of crummy looking, I have to admit, with worn-out motel-style furniture, but completely adequate. In the apartment next door, two or three lifestyle trainers, LSTs as they were called, would be monitoring the residents' quarters every hour or so—even throughout the night. Rachel was assigned a roommate, an older woman who'd suffered a stroke. Residents like Rachel would learn to shop for their own food and prepare their own meals as well as receive daily therapies and, eventually, work in the community. It was too good to be true.

But, for a while, it was true. After a three-day weekend, I flew back alone to Salt Lake with only a little trepidation. Rachel would be cared for by people who knew how to care for her, and I would be free. I felt the liberation flood my body like a drug. The trials of the past few years slid away almost entirely. Light as air, I took up my University job, I counseled students, I wrote fiction. I was no longer dead-weight in the department: My workload of committees had expanded to enormous proportions. I was now serving on twenty-six Ph.D. and M.F.A. committees, the department's executive and graduate committees, and a hiring committee for a new fiction writer, of which I was the chair. I was over-worked, but happy to be so.

Rachel missed me; of course, she missed me. She called collect daily and sometimes twice a day with complaints. Prime among these, as usual, were complaints about the other brain injured and how she was humiliated to be "grouped with them." I listened and cajoled. When I hung up, I felt twinges of guilt mixed with relief.

I visited the program several times during Rachel's five-month stay and was generally heartened. Thanks to a truly gifted neuropsychologist, Ray McBride, Rachel had finally been put on Ritalin, which produced almost miraculous results. Her short-term memory had taken a giant step forward. Now she was able to hold a vague picture of each day's noteworthy events in her head. She would remember, for example, a bad therapy session; she would remember an exchange with some-one she liked. Best of all, she was less antsy.

My friend Connie, who accompanied me on one of my

visits, noticed immediately that Rachel was able to sustain a dinner table conversation without jumping up to do the dishes. She actually listened to subject matter that did not include her. The dinner had been prepared by Rachel— chicken fajitas and a Caesar salad—and she'd invited her favorite LST, Bev (whom Rachel called "Veb"), to meet me, the Matcha Casserole-head Girlfriend Jones.

That visit, I accompanied her to a therapy session with Ray McBride, and she stunned me by taking notes of what they spoke about during the meeting. Progress on all fronts. Her physical therapy was going very well; she was standing straighter and walking more sturdily than before. She was losing weight. She was working out. The complaining, however, continued. In fact, she seemed to be more volatile than I'd seen her be in a while.

It turns out that the physiatrist, Dr. Waterman, had taken her off Depakote. Thus the weight loss. Thus, also, I told him via Ray McBride, the volatility. Personally, I could never seem to arrange a real meeting with Dr. Waterman, a man I'd met once and who remains a pale blur in my mind. I'd hear back, for example, that the Depakote was not causing her mood swings, but that the moodiness was adjustment related. No, I'd say to the secretary or lifestyle trainer or Ray McBride, it's the lack of Depakote. Rachel doesn't have adjustment problems—and, in any case, why would adjustment suddenly be a problem, three months post–program entry, coincident with her being taken off Depakote? During that trip, she had a mild tremor attack that I was sure was a small seizure activated by the lack of Depakote. Again, Dr. Waterman told me via someone-or-other that it wasn't a seizure. When I arrived back in Salt Lake, I tried repeatedly to get him on the phone, but no luck.

After Rachel went off Depakote, the news from Ray of Hope was always mixed. Accompanied by a lifestyle trainer, she was tutoring a few students at the local high school. The reports on her interactions with students, her focus on the material, were generally positive. But then she had had a "fit" on her way to the tutoring session, had hit the LST repeatedly on the arm during the drive, had shrieked in the high school corridors. "Get her back on Depakote," I'd say in a voice that sounded dull even to my ears.

So she moved into a small apartment with two room-mates who, in exchange for a break in the rent, were to be Rachel's new buddies and helpers. Not her caretakers. She lived across from the Y, and every day she'd betake herself there and ride the stationary bike. But the roommate situation worsened along with Rachel's mood swings. In late July, I received a phone call from the director of the re-entry organization. They hadn't been able to find a job for Rachel, mainly on account of her resistance to career-path suggestions; and the roommates were "throwing in the towel." "What do you suggest?" I asked the director, a woman I'd met once before. "I suggest she return home to you," she said, adding that there was no facility, no nursing home, no nothing that would accept Rachel in her current condition.

Two days later, Rachel flew into Salt Lake. She looked great. The daily workouts at the Y had made her almost athletic-looking again. She was standing straighter; her memory, though still most imperfect, was functioning enough to keep her focused; and she'd lost weight. I'd put in a call to Dr.

Gray in Tucson, who recommended strongly that she get back on Depakote, and I had the prescription waiting when Rachel arrived. Two days later, she was a calm girl.

Her Ray of Hope experience had been mostly positive, but I still blame the physiatrist for its disappointing outcome. Now she was in Utah where there were no resources like Ray of Hope, where for the next year she'd walk around and around the neighborhood, indulging her Cucina habit, putting on weight. And I'd worry again.

Though not as much. I'd become casual about Rachel's wanderings, and now, when I received the occasional phone call from a stranger, I no longer flinched. Rachel, it seemed, was known to everyone in town. She had angels watching her. At the opening of the mega-health food store in Salt Lake, a day during which hundreds of people walked shoulder-to-shoulder in the long nutritiously packed aisles, the young, nose-pierced checkout man asked me, "Are you Rachel's mother?"

I was taken aback. "How do you know Rachel?"

He smiled widely. "Everyone knows Rachel."

THAT YEAR, I'D RESUMED seeing my pre-accident psychotherapist, a wonderful, funny, sympathetic man named Arthur. We talked about Rachel, naturally, but we also talked about me. I had a sabbatical coming up for 2000–2001, and I wanted to go somewhere, do something. I wanted to write without student phone calls and quasiprofessional obligations. I wanted to leave Salt Lake City and go to San Miguel for a year. But, I explained to Arthur, it would be impossible.

"I don't see what's so impossible," said Arthur from his calm perch on the chair facing mine.

Are you kidding? Mexico, cobbled streets, a year, my new house, my book contract, Rachel's stationary bike (staff of life), medications, doctors, family, money, students, committees—I went on and on with my objections.

Arthur smiled happily. "Sounds great to me." (He has a habit of glomming onto the positive in our conversations.) His eyes looked almost dreamy as he leaned back in his chair and imagined (I imagined him imagining) Rachel and me in Mexico.

I got the picture.

"Write me a letter," he said. "You'll have a blast."

Epilogue: San Miguel

. . . and yes, I've learned how to shake shake shake the bootay to the salsa beat & even in the heat — & with my right side's refusal to go with the flow, I've learned, dang knabbit, that I can still put on a show . . .

—Rachel's journal, 2001

It's Saturday morning, early March. Cool, sunny, blue. Last night it rained unseasonable torrents, rain spilling from the open-mouthed *canales* onto the roofs of the colonial homes, rain racing down the cobbles. In the moonlight, the stone-slabbed sidewalks shone green and gold.

Rachel, who has lived in her own apartment for a month now, made her way through the storm to see me. I hadn't been feeling well, and on the phone she'd said, "I think you need me to come and baby you." It was a comforting idea. I'd throw in baked potatoes for the two of us, maybe burgers. This was around five P.M. and it hadn't yet begun to rain.

But then she forgot, or got waylaid, or went the wrong

way. Eventually, she showed up in the middle of the storm. I was in the living room, and I heard her voice from the street, calling "MOM! MOM!" at the top of her lungs. I slipped a coat over my pj's (I *was* sick) and saw her silhouette up the dark road, inching down the narrow and slippery sidewalk, swearing loudly. For some reason—maybe the cold—her right arm had seized up at the elbow and her hand was scraping along the buildings' rough edges, hurting her. "I can't even see," she said when I reached her.

I slipped my arm around her waist and took her cane in my left hand. In this manner, we made our way to the door of my apartment, Rachel on the sidewalk and me on the cobbled street below, holding onto her. As we walked, she regaled me in the way she does when she's frustrated.

"This," she said with vehemence, almost stumbling, "is just one more example of my fucking life."

"Never mind about your fucking life. Keep walking," I said.

Once inside she shed her wet clothes and put on a Nike T-shirt of mine and a red sweater. Then she walked to the kitchen to check out its state of repair. Unlike hers, mine always has a few dishes in the sink, a few crumbs on the counters. She looks forward to it. She offers an analysis, which is this: Before brain injury, she, Rachel, was the usual sloppy athlete, right? Right. But tidying up the kitchen (we dub her "Tidy Spice" these days) is Rachel's way of completing something, of experiencing the satisfaction that comes from reaching a goal: a kind of narrative impulse, now that I think of it.

"It's like running," she tells me. "In a weird way, believe it or not, Mom, cleaning the kitchen is my running substitute."

Last night, in the kitchen, she sang: "Tidy Spice likes everything nice."

"That's your little theme song," I said. She walked from tiled counter to tiled counter with a sponge. I watched from the couch, reclining, my hands behind my head, which still ached.

I say she *walks*. These days she leaves the cane at the door and walks on her own, a little lopsided, through any familiar dwelling. I wish she'd walk without her cane all the time, everywhere, I tell her, but we both agree the cane is good insurance on the San Miguel cobbles and skinny, irregular sidewalks. In her own digs, she leaves the cane propped up on a dining room chair, which is how I know she's home this morning when I look through her plate-glass door.

"Is it you, Girlfriend?" she says in her joyous, happy-to-see-me voice. She's upstairs reading our friend Tony Cohan's *On Mexican Time*, a lovely, lyrical account of his and his wife Masako's adventures in San Miguel. I've brought Rache some milk and some pesos for the day. I don't know what she'll do or even if she has a plan. But I'll be writing.

WE ARRIVED IN San Miguel in late July, dragging no fewer than eight large duffels-on-wheels, my computer, and a few backpacks. We'd actually been bumped to a first-class flight from Los Angeles to León, a mirror image of my painful first-class flight to Denver five years ago, when Rachel was comatose and near death. ("I had a near-death experience," she tells everyone, as a prelude to her story.) Then, to complete the déjà vu, we ensconced ourselves in the very same flat where I received the phone call that changed my life in

August 1995. There were seven other flats, but I chose this one, not only for its charming ambiance—a view of the San Miguel hills and the lake from the flower-filled balcony—but because I wanted to believe we'd come full circle, that by ending where we'd begun, we were concluding this particular narrative and, thus, giving a shape to our lives.

The flat is situated in a five-hundred-year-old colonial house in the center of San Miguel. As in the style of colonial homes, the individual flats surround a large stone courtyard with a fountain in the middle and a few wrought-iron tables and chairs for guest lounging. It is a communal place, still presided over by Toni Gerez, an eighty-something writer and translator with a taste for the absurd and the bohemian.

Toni took to Rachel immediately, and vice versa. Often I'd hear them in the courtyard from our own upstairs flat, laughing and talking. "What does this mean, *it sucks*," Toni would ask Rachel, half-disingenuously, and they'd be off on a river of associations, Toni madly scribbling down Rachel-wisdom, as I call it—my daughter's penchant for the offbeat remark, which nonetheless hits the mark, like poetry.

From Toni's, we had easy access to the Jardin, the central square where gringo and nongringo mingle, smoke cigarettes, and gaze at the Paroquia, the most spectacular of San Miguel's cathedrals; to little tiendas which sell milk, cigarettes, fresh vegetables; to shops full of seductive tourist trash; to cafes where black-eyed waitresses amiably take Rachel's order and detailed instructions for the perfect iced mocha.

Right away, Rachel walked everywhere—such a change from our two-week trip in '97! She walks slowly, carefully, talking to children and señoras along the way in her flawless

Spanish. (I usually raced ahead—too many conversational detours, and my Spanish sucks.) The few destinations outside her reach were available to her by taxi, and soon most taxi drivers knew her by name, shouting, as one did two days ago, *Hola Raquel!* from his window as he sped by.

"She's a people magnet," a friend noted, observing, no doubt, Rachel holding forth in the Jardin, switching effortlessly from Spanish to English, joking in both languages, or swinging her cane to the music of mariachis or the Cuban salsa band that toured here last fall. This maneuver, a theatrical attention-grabber, is occasionally dangerous to any in the vicinity: the cane upended and twirling in the air above her head and Rachel rotating her hips (her rhythm's back), "shaking her bootay," as in the old days.

I call them "the old days" now, though in many ways, the old days seem to have returned to us here in Mexico. It is as if we've traveled a million miles—in time, in emotional energy—only to land in our spot, where we are both immeasurably at home. Rachel has resumed her painting, taking advantage of the art classes at the Instituto and Bellas Artes. She paints from that sureness of instinct, unmarred by self-consciousness, that all artists strive for. Perhaps this is the result of using her left, nondominant hand. Perhaps it's brain injury disinhibition, from which she still suffers. I watch as she places a line of blue around a yellow background. At the painting's center is a high-heeled Nike, red and green, with the signature white swirl on the side. This, her latest, is a whimsical piece, its title *Heels, Nike* scrawled across the top in black paint. Is the framed unlikely Nike—her brand-of-choice running shoe way back when—Rachel's way of parking that old life solidly in the past? I'm hoping it is.

She's excited about this book and has, along the way, been my faithful reader and listener. She wishes I wouldn't mention her weight, which is still a problem, but everything else is okay with her, though she's suggested modifying the subtitle to "A Story of Memory, Survival, and a Multitude of Chin Hairs" (also true). On a more serious note, she says, "I'm sorry I put you through so much, Mom," leading me to worry that I've made myself a martyr in these pages, which would be far from the truth. Because it is Rachel, always, who is the valiant one, who persists through her still-foggy short-term memory, her occasional mood swings, her physical limitations—none of which will ever vanish completely. We know this now. But her amazing spirit, of which I am in awe, always, will not vanish either.

In September, we traveled to San Francisco for Geoff's wedding. After the celebration, a most graceful accomplishment by Geoff's beautiful bride Jennifer, the plan was that Rachel go to Tucson to try to begin a new life. She'd return with stepfather John and live with him until she found a job—perhaps, I was hoping, at Bentley's. She lasted three weeks and then begged to come back to San Miguel. Without transportation and far from her usual Tucson haunts, she was lost. And Bentley's, which does a bustling business behind the counter (to put it mildly), turned out to be no place for a girl with a cane and the use of one, non-dominant hand. (How could we have thought so?)

Whereas San Miguel is a place where everyone walks around, just like Rachel. Where people look forward to meeting new friends in the Jardin and the little cafes surrounding it. Where life is leisurely and somehow more humane without cars and shopping malls. Instead, parades abound—I hear one now outside my window, a clear horn blaring two notes and the *rat-tat-tat* of drumbeats fading out of sound—and fireworks spray the night sky without reason.

I do not want to romanticize. Rachel seems to do better here than elsewhere—the ambiance accommodates her ebullient spirit. But whether she will be able to make real friends, whether she will be able to find a job, manage money, ever have access to the full, rich shape of each day and carry it forward to the next, I don't know.

At times, the signs seem hopeful. Last week she met a young man in the Jardin who asked her to lunch for the following day. Though she'd neglected to jot down his name, she dutifully noted the date and the time. Her hunch, she told me, was that, though he was quite handsome, he was gay. "A gay man trapped in a totally hot body," she'd quipped the night before. On the "date," they'd gone somewhere to eat—Rachel could remember neither place nor food—and talked for an hour or so about his relationship with his partner. "So I was right!" Rachel announced triumphantly, words which revealed access to her recovering short-term memory, music to my ears.

On the other hand, she didn't remember where I lived two short days ago and wandered for hours in search of a familiar landmark. (I heard this not from Rachel, but from a friend who came upon her fast dissolving in confusion and tears.) And this afternoon, she lost the peso equivalent of twenty bucks—who knows where? Now, however, as opposed to a month ago, such failings upset her, suggesting what? Perhaps the return of accountability.

In October, we moved into new digs next to Toni's. A fortuitous find, our little flat had two bedrooms and even a rooftop garden overlooking the city. Then, in December, our friend Laura invited me to take over her flat, two blocks away. Laura would be spending the next four months in London. Thus our new plan, now in action: I have moved, Rachel is on her own. We have a "maid" who comes three days a week to cook and clean for Rachel. Only in Mexico can one afford such luxuries for thirty dollars a week.

Years ago—who knows when this occurred in the meandering Rachel saga?—one of our many psychologists advised that when I got on with my own life, Rachel would get on with hers. "You have to begin the process," I was told. "She's not going to until you do." It made little sense to me at the time, because really, wasn't I living my own life and taking care of Rachel? What did this mean, *living my own life?* Honestly, I couldn't conceive of it.

But when Laura made her offer, I began to see my small window of opportunity. I envisioned sitting on this very chair, the long shuttered windows open and letting in the sunlight, writing, as I am now, uninterrupted, Laura's cats, Blue and Pandora, curled up beside me. I see now that I had to break a long habit of servitude with Rachel. Little things, like getting her the salt or a glass of water or a jacket, tasks which she can easily perform on her own; reminding her to take her meds, instead of insisting that she remember; doling out money which she'd spend and which I'd replenish, without consequences.

My move away has not been easy on Rachel, especially initially. In the beginning of February, she wept every day for a week, complaining bitterly to her brothers and sister long distance that I'd "abandoned" her. "I don't understand why we have to live apart, Girlfriend," she'd say to me, weeping.

"Because this is the next step," I'd say. "This is where we both have to go next."

We're still in an experimental stage, I caution myself, when the sheer bliss of living alone teases me into thinking that all our problems are solved. As my sabbatical draws to a close in early August, I will return to Salt Lake for good, whereas plans for Rachel are contingent. I would like her to stay here in San Miguel, and it *is* feasible, actually, since we are surrounded by caring friends and inexpensive help. But will she be ready by August to take on her own life? Will the job at the bilingual school work out? Will she be able to create a social life fulfilling enough to sustain her? And even if I can afford to come to San Miguel every few months, will she be able to exist on her own without me? Because now, at this stage of recovery, it's become clear to me that the real challenge Rachel faces is the human one. "You are Rachel's buffer against the world," an insightful friend told me a year ago. "Get out of her way."

In the past month, Rachel has made a giant leap forward. Now, we eat dinner together and generally cross paths in the morning. Our time together is, as they say, quality time. We have real conversations. The other evening, over bowls of pasta in a wonderful Italian restaurant, we discussed the esoteric implications of Rachel's brain injury and recovery.

"Remember how you always thought this would happen to you?" I asked her.

"I do remember," she said, and we grin because it's a happy feat, still, for Rachel to remember anything from her post-accident life. "It seems it was always in the back of my mind. Since I was a kid."

And I remind her that I knew it too, that I'd always had a

remote vision of this time with Rachel. "Our karma," I told her. "I mean, Rache, don't you think it's possible your soul chose this?"

Rachel looks dubious, as she should. But I can't help entertaining this notion as I recall the pre-accident Rachel in all her young adult wisdom, "the perfect child," who, from the point of view of the soul, possibly had it too easy. And me too, in my melancholy boredom.

"Still, Mom"—she calls me "Mom" now that we've split apart, which feels much righter to me than all the goofy nicknames—"we've showed those doctors." Indeed, for her, as well as for me, Dr. Frank's gloomy prediction that Rachel would never lead an independent life looms large, especially in this experimental phase. We would both like to think we've showed those doctors. We have tried to.

Things happen for a reason, people say, as if a reason could remedy a tragedy. And yet, when I write that word, *tragedy,* I balk at its incompleteness, its failure to take into account the *gloriment*—another Rachel word, conveying both the exuberance of her being and its pathos. Indeed, no conversation is invulnerable to her sideways and slantwise interpretations, or *not not* doubled, or somehow, as she's said, "skewed to the left"—as if the whole joke of the thing winds up being life's outrageousness, which is neither rational nor tragic.

And so, as in her running career, Rachel is rising to the task of her independence. This is the way she's always been—she needs the challenge dangling carrotlike in front of her in order to move forward. I think now of that early time when it seemed as if she'd stay hooked up to a ventilator forever. But then she was gradually weaned. Deprived of artificial breaths, she breathed. Deprived of the trach tube, she breathed. Deprived of the mother as caregiver, Rachel, I pray, will breathe full, *gloriment* breaths, taking in her freedom and her new life.

We have come full circle in another, most crucial way. Here, in the heart of Guadalupe territory, our new friend is Bev Donofrio, whose latest memoir *Looking for Mary* is a tribute to the Virgin's power. (A coincidence? A miracle?) Indeed, I not only feel Guadalupe's holy presence with special intensity here, but see her image everywhere, the patron Virgin of Mexico, whose roots extend further back than Christianity, into the figures of Aztec goddesses. "Just ask her," says Bev, astonishingly confident, "and she'll give you what you need." So we do. We will. And she has.

How much of human personality is a matter of neurons and axons and chemicals? *How much of you remains, my darling?* The young woman who won races and shoved her way around international airports? Not her, but not *not* her either. Who is she now? This trillion-dollar question has become almost irrelevant here in the beautiful face of whoever she is on this March morning in San Miguel, five and a half years post-injury, when the tree outside my window (*a small but detailed tree*) is blazing and twirling against a sky the same color as her eyes, which (unlike mine) are clear of tears.

———

Dear Rachel: This final paragraph is for you. You've given me the most profound experience of my life. I haven't always been kind, I haven't always been patient, but I have never faltered in my faith in you. You are the most courageous person I will ever know. You are my inspiration. Let me remind you of a conversation I happened to jot down in one of my many note-books, the ones I keep losing. You said, "Dare to be different," and I said, "What's that supposed to mean?"

"I like the alliteration so very much."

"Yes, but do you like the sentiment?"

"The *scentiment*—you mean it's a little stinky?"

And I said, "Oh ha ha ha, a pun. But what about dare to be different?"

And you said, "I say right on. I'm living proof of it, am I not?" That says it all.

ACKNOWLEDGMENTS

THIS BOOK COULD never have been written without the love, encouragement, and support of my children, Rachel's siblings, Margot and Steve Kerr, Chris Brennan, Geoff and Jennifer Brennan; my father, Bud Morley, whose unexpected death occurred tragically in the middle of Rachel's recovery and whom we miss more than we can say; my mother, Margot Morley, whose constant prayers have done more than any therapy session could; my sister, Mary Pat, my brother Billy and, especially, my brother Jim, who, time after time, listened patiently and compassionately to all my woes and helped me see more clearly; Tom Brennan,

Rachel's dad, and John Palumbo, Rachel's stepdad, who was always there for us.

I am grateful, also, for the sympathy and friendship of the countless doctors, nurses, therapists, and health care workers along the way—especially Eloise from Denver, Louise, Sue, Denise, and Cat, Rachel's great nurse Pat, and the wonderful, inspiring Dr. Judy Gooch and Dr. Eric Hansen.

Thanks also to Rachel's many friends, notably Bridget Smythe, Uma Paniker, Mark Levin, Stacey Peterson, Gene Marsh, and Karen Sahn, who have stuck with her through the long haul; to my dear friends and ICU vigil keepers Toni Nelson, Robin Hiller, and Beth Alvarado; to Rachel's Utah team, Srinivas Aravamudan, Ranji Khanna, Tom Stillinger, Meg Brady, Kathryn Stockton, Jackie Osherow, and Shelley White; and to my pals Mark Doty, Paul Lisicky, David Nelson, Donald Revell, Claudia Keelan, Aga Shahid Ali, all of the Warren Wilson crew, especially Pete Turchi and Emily Labatto, Arden Lubek, Jane Miller, Barbara Culley, Kim Westerman, and Frances Shoberg, and Charlie Baxter; and for special love in the down times, Sue Chartrand, Connie Voisine, Michael Schwalb, Wendy Rawlings, Cathy Wagner, and Martin Corless-Smith.

For our wonderful year in San Miguel, I am grateful to Dr. Arthur Traub, who made me believe we could do it. Also special heartfelt gratitude to San Miguel pals Tony Cohan, Michela Emeson, Masako Takahashi, Bev Donofrio, Suzanne Kimball, Sashi Kimball, Mark van Lokerran, Paul Duffy, and, for the music, Tyler Mitchell.

I couldn't have completed this manuscript without the support of my department chair, Charles Berger, and the last-minute technical expertise of the amazing Sheila Olson.

A special thanks to Elizabeth Wales for her belief in me. And to Carol Houck Smith for her wise and careful attention to this book.

And to the Virgin of Guadalupe, for listening to our prayers.